A Sailor's Tales

by

Captain William Wells
Master Mariner

Critical Book Reviews

In spite of the title hinting this is a 'boy's book', it is not! As a woman, mother and grandmother, from start to finish I enjoyed this very readable book. With all its twists and turns, to my surprise I found I could just not put it down.

Mrs Sally Hart JP Oxford

This is at times quite a humorous book which follows the life path of a very interesting character, one who really has led a full life. We recommend this book as suitable reading for all.

Yorkshire Post

This book is recommended as a good and interesting read.

The Times

"A Sailors Tales" is a gripping read – and not only to those having an interest in the sea. Recommended.

The Mail

Well done Cap'n. A darn good and enjoyable yarn!

The New Zealand Herald, Auckland, New Zealand

This is the story of a local boy who made good overseas. Whilst he was still a schoolboy here in Wellington, young Billy Wells won a scholarship and left for England from where he spent the majority of his life sailing the great oceans of the world. His autobiographical book *"A Sailor's Tales"* tells of his almost 50 years at sea and of the many adventures he encountered along the way.

The Dominion Post, Wellington, New Zealand

I write to congratulate you and thank you for a very interesting read. Serving on the Board of the Steamship Historical Society of America, I have more than 5,000 pieces of liner ephemera in my collection and over 300 books. *"A Sailor's Tales"* now occupies a prized place in my library. I've come to realise over the past several years that contemporary histories are far more engaging than armchair histories written long after the fact and your book brilliantly illustrates that point. Well done!

Richard Rabbett. Steamship Historical Society of America, Boston, Massachusetts

110 days short of completing 49 years at sea Captain William Wells retired. In this autobiographical account lies the story of an interesting career at sea, latterly as a Trinity House pilot and now as a Public Speaker. Captain Wells' personality shines through his story which is punctuated with his sense of humour and some frank speaking at times. From the very first chapter, his enthusiasm for his career at sea is apparent and his enthusiasm for the subject draws the reader through this appealing read.

Horizon, Trinity House's magazine

It is said that everybody has at least one book in them, and after spending almost 49 years at sea, retired Master Mariner Captain William Wells has decided to write one. This book *"A Sailor's Tales"* tells about his life at sea, then as a harbour pilot, serving in the Middle East, Bahamas and the Port of London and since retirement he has become recognised as an internationally acclaimed public speaker and lecturer on 'matters maritime'.

The result is a masterful account which contains many anecdotes about his travels and his adventures. Pursuing an almost compulsive relationship with his mistress the sea, this book can be described as Wells' 'cruise of a lifetime'. Hurricanes, stowaways, the Biafra civil war and the eccentricities of life at sea are all covered here and written in an easy light hearted and humorous way.

Lloyds List, the International Shipping Daily Newspaper. Founded in 1734 and distributed throughout 100 different countries, world-wide.

Looking through your website I came to the page about your book which inspired me to purchase a copy. What a super story you have to tell and congratulations for telling it in such an interesting and captivating manner.

Rear Admiral Bob Esquivel Acapulco, Mexico

I first heard an interview with Captain William Wells by Libby Purves on BBC Radio 4's 'Midweek' programme just before Christmas and learning about his book entitled *"A Sailor's Tales"* went out straightaway and purchased a copy. Captain Wells' story was most interesting to listen to on the radio as well as reading it in his book.

Jason Cummerfield, Nautical Institute, London.

This is a thoroughly enjoyable read of the life and career of a professional Master Mariner turned professional public speaker. I found this book well written in an easy manner and needed to turn the page to find what was coming next! This book illustrates the life of Captain Wells which is quite different from the majority of the population, and in places I found myself quite envious. We unreservedly recommend this book to all.

The Blackwell Bookshop online

This is a fascinating account of one man's remarkable career. It is at once an informative, sometimes humorous glimpse into the maritime world. I enjoyed it immensely.

Dr Carolyn A Rhodes

I have known, I have sailed and worked ashore with Captain William Wells for many years and have seen at first hand his consummate professionalism, so I read his book *"A Sailor's Tales"* with great interest. A sailor, not a writer, he has nevertheless managed to make his book informative, interesting and in many places very funny. I would recommend this publication to anyone interested in following the career path, with all its twists and turns, of a truly remarkable and professional Master Mariner.

Capt. John McBride Trinity House, London

Authentic and well-written stories of life at sea are relatively rare. Many ignore the social implications for the family left behind and very few recount experiences encountered onshore whilst abroad. But this book written by Master Mariner, Captain William Wells entitled *"A Sailor's Tales"* deals with all these aspects which is a fine account taking the reader on a fascinating voyage through an experienced captain's life as well as when he comes ashore to work as a Harbour Pilot. The book, which details the life and work of someone dedicated to a most unusual occupation, deserves a wide audience.

Philip Algar, Author and Broadcaster

Retired seafarer, Captain William Wells who throughout his long career at sea encountered war, dodged rocket propelled grenades, witnessed murder, sailed through two full blown hurricanes and experienced one hundred and one other adventures, has finally recalled them all in an autobiographical account entitled *"A Sailor's Tales"*.

Throughout the pages of his book comes this stark message, which in his own words are: *"I am one of those few people in the world who has actually lived my boyhood dream; my life has been a ball"*

Northampton Chronicle & Echo

This book tells the life story of a young New Zealander who having won a scholarship to travel to England for basic nautical training soon embarked on his life-long career at sea. Never thinking of what he was doing was 'work', half a century later his continued enthusiasm for his career still shines through.

There is something endlessly fascinating about reading and listening to someone who loves their job and is very good at it. They have the ability to explain, without any jargon, what it is they did and why, as well as including many humorous and not so humorous anecdotes.

This is a man who is rightly proud of all he has achieved in his life, but this is not a book of self-praise. After retirement Captain Wells turned to full-time Public Speaking and has devoted his considerable knowledge and enthusiasms to informing and bringing pleasure to his numerous audiences. It was a great pleasure and enjoyment to review this book.

For a full review of this book go to:
www.thebookbag.com/bookreviews. **The Book Bag**

A Sailor's Tales
by
Captain William Wells

2nd Edition 2012

ISBN: 978-0-9562904-0-3

Published by Captain William Wells in conjunction with Writersworld Ltd

Printed and bound by
www.printondemand-worldwide.com

www.writersworld.co.uk

WRITERSWORLD
2 Bear Close
Woodstock
Oxfordshire
OX20 1JX
England

To my best friend, my confidante, my wife: Diana, who is one of the very few people in the entire world who truly understands me and what drove me in my career at sea. Without her at my side helping, encouraging, offering constructive criticism where appropriate, my post retirement career or writing this book would never have been possible. Thank you.

Contents

Preamble

As I sit here at home in my study, looking out across the snow laden countryside of Northamptonshire, probably as far removed from the sea as one can be in this country, I like to reflect over the years - the countless adventures willingly and unwillingly encountered, and the hundreds of thousands of miles my life journey has travelled. I cannot help but wonder where I would have been today had I followed my original intentions of returning to my native New Zealand.

As a boy, I would spend hours gazing out of my bedroom window in Wellington watching the ships as they sailed out from the Harbour only to disappear over the horizon where the sea met the sky. I was smitten by a curiosity in what might be there when you reached the horizon, for it didn't dawn on me, until I was a seaman myself, that the horizon was never actually reached; simply because there is no such definitive thing.

I spent the first five years of my sea-going career sailing mainly on the European/American/ Australasian routes. It had been my intention, when I qualified as a ship's officer and navigator, to return home and sail the seven seas from there, aboard New Zealand flagged ships. But...I saw the state of this country - this wonderful United Kingdom, and thought that, seeing as you had trained me, the least I could do was to stay here and help you out. So I did. I took your jobs, paid your taxes, helped your breweries stay in business and I even chased and married your women! And here I am many decades later, still here, and I still like to think I am helping you out...well at least I can still manage to pay the taxes!

It is true that I have had a long, successful and many have said "distinguished" career at sea, lasting

110 days short of 49 years. I am often asked, as I now travel around the country delivering talks and lectures, why, if only for round figures, did I not stay on for those extra 110 days or even, one year and 110 days? The answer is simple: the circle had been completed. For I had now done my fair share and it was time go and move on, allowing the next generation of seafarers to carry on where I left off.

I can truthfully say that my life has been a ball. In my eyes I have never had a 'proper' job, for I felt I was just a simple sailor, and what you see was what you got. Best of all I was, for almost 36 years, allowed to 'play' with someone else's ship as a commercial marine pilot. It was good fun to be able to say to a ship's captain, with one's tongue deeply embedded in one's cheek, "*Well captain, whatever I do wrong, is your fault*". On a more serious note it was a great feeling to have an experienced captain say, after a particularly difficult piece of piloting and manoeuvring, "*Thank you pilot. Nice job and well done*". To be considered professionally as a 'safe, steady and secure pair of hands' is probably one of the greatest accolades any pilot can be given.

Every ship being brought into or sailing from a port, or being moved from one part of the port to another, under the guidance of a licensed pilot for that port, is undertaking what is known as 'an act of Pilotage'. Every pilot, like the airline pilot who counts up the hours flown, keeps a log of every 'act of Pilotage' they have performed. By the time I had retired as the Senior River Pilot in the Port of London, my tally had risen to a total of 8,153 'acts of Pilotage' as a licensed pilot, on more than 5,000 different ships, and I can truthfully say that I was still learning, even on my last trip down the River Thames.

Chapter 1

Growing up in New Zealand

What normal schoolboy, anywhere in the world, likes the confines of the classroom when there is a big wide world outside just waiting to be explored, and especially if that world included the open wharves and those ships lying in the port of Wellington, New Zealand's capital city?

I was no exception to that rule. Sports mad and good enough to play for Wellington Province in rugby and cricket, as well as being a reasonably competent tennis player, my sporting fixtures and practices, plus the lure of the open waterfront, were far more attractive to me than the tedium of the English lessons which the dreaded Miss McGraith struggled in vain to teach me.

Academia, with the exception of those sciences that actually interested me, held no place in the life of Billy Wells. For I was a young man, a boy really, who knew what I wanted and where I was going in life, even when still aged only 14 - it was a life at sea for me and nothing else mattered. Living and acting it out as a 'pretend life' made it seem all very simple – if only I knew what I was letting myself in for! How many times later in my life would that statement "if only I knew..." arise?

It was not that I hated school but the majority of my teachers never inspired me, nor I think, understood me! I could not get them to realise that I simply was not interested in verbs, adjectives etc., or what William Shakespeare did with his life and the beauty (?!) of the words he wrote. Perhaps that's the reason why I received only 2% for English Language in New Zealand's equivalent of an 'O' level paper. If I had to attend school, and let's face it, the law said I did, the subjects that held my interest, apart from the way they were taught, were geography, maths and physics. They made sense to me and I could understand them; for me, here was the real beauty - that was not words, but numbers and symbols.

I was born into an old and established New Zealand family, with both my parents as well as three grandparents having been born there. My father was a respected member of the local community who ran his own carpentry business and expected his only son to carry on the family-named company. He used all his persuasive powers to deter me from a headlong flight into a seafaring career. But what he never realised was that I had little or no aptitude, or interest, plus ten left thumbs when it came to woodwork.

Reaching the age of 15, I went behind my parents' back and applied for a scholarship that enabled six boys each year free travel from New Zealand to the UK, where they would undertake their basic nautical training before being let loose to go to sea. This scholarship was a joint venture between the British Sailors' Society, a Christian based international organisation caring for the welfare of seamen of any nationality and creed, and the P&O Shipping Line with one of its major subsidiary companies, the New Zealand Shipping Co. (NZS, as it was known throughout the shipping world), both of which had their head offices in London.

Both my parents and school teachers alike smiled at the thought of Billy Wells sitting anything as academic as a scholarship, least of all one so restrictive that only six were issued each year throughout the entire land. They thought the best course of action was to humour me and so, having received a somewhat grudging approval, the big day came about in September 1956 when, surprisingly confident, I entered the examination room. You can imagine the reaction when, a few weeks later, the results were published and I received the 2nd highest score of the 20 or so candidates, from throughout all of New Zealand, who applied for and sat the examination.

My elder sister was married on a fine sunny summer Saturday in February 1957 and the following Thursday my parents accompanied me on the overnight sleeper train from Wellington to Auckland. This was where I was to join the ship *m.v. Hurunui* which was to take me away from my homeland and family and deliver me to England. I had just turned sixteen years of age, one month earlier. I am sure that my mother was devastated that, within one week, she had lost both her eldest daughter and only son. But with the arrogance or, was it perhaps ignorance, of teenage youth, coupled with the fact that I was terribly ambitious, I was not perhaps as sensitive to the family changes as maybe I should have been.

m.v. HURUNUI

After a few delays we finally sailed from Auckland bound for the Panama Canal, the Caribbean island of Curacao, Genoa and finally Liverpool - we had to go the 'long way' to Italy, because in early 1957 the Suez Canal was still closed to all shipping, caused by the Suez crisis the previous year. The combination of a few days of homesickness and seasickness could not dampen my spirits, as I realised, quite naively I suppose, that one day the shipping company would actually pay me a salary to do what I was now doing for free.

However, arriving in Liverpool on a cold damp misty day in March 1957, and seeing for the first time in my life rows upon rows of terraced housing, was such a culture shock. For one fleeting moment I wondered whether I had made the right decision in leaving the wide-open spaces of New Zealand for cramped and overcrowded England.

Chapter 2

Basic Training and early days at sea

It is an old adage that school days are the best days of your life...Really? I did not think so, but during those days at the nautical training establishment in Dover, England, I blossomed in a way I never thought possible. Top of Lancing class in 1957 and a candidate for the Captain Superintendent's sword of that year, I'd never realised learning could be so much fun! The difference now, of course, was that I was learning what I really wanted to know.

At the Prince of Wales Sea Training School, Dover, we were under the guidance of our Captain Superintendent Commander John Hough DSC RD and it was our tutors, Commander Joe Hadley RNR, Charlie Porter and William (Sludge) Smith to name but three, who made learning such FUN whilst at the same time installing into us raw recruits a sense of responsibility and pride in the service in which some of us would dedicate much of our lives.

Several years later, in 2005, the PWSTS celebrated the 75th anniversary of its founding, by the then Prince of Wales. I was invited to be the Guest Speaker, and old boys and their wives and partners attended from all over the world. In many ways it was quite an eye opener to realise when the eight of us 'old boys' from the Lancing Class of 1957 gathered together, that only one was still serving at sea. And you can probably guess who that was? Apart from myself, not one of my former classmates had spent many years at sea. Most had married, 'swallowed the anchor' and found some form of employment ashore. I could not help but wonder if they had been as happy in their work ashore as I had been in mine at sea.

The months spent at Dover sped by so fast. We were proudly on display at the marching out ceremony without fully realising how far we had all progressed. We were sent out from the training establishment as senior cadets, unaware that another shock awaited us - we soon found ourselves nothing more than very lowly junior worms when we joined our first ship.

The NZS had two ships of their fleet dedicated to the training of both deck and engineering officers. These ships - *m.v. Durham* and *m.v. Rakai* - were manned by specialist training officers and engineers and, apart from the regular Petty Officers, the remainder of the crew were made up of would-be officers and engineers. But for some inexplicable reason the Company preferred to appoint their young antipodean Midshipmen, not to one of their 'cadet ships' but to the ordinary ships of the fleet, more often than not those trading between Europe and North America to Australia and New Zealand. This enabled us teenagers to regularly visit our homes and families.

Ignoring the passage from New Zealand to England, my first trip to sea was aboard the New Zealand Shipping Company's passenger liner *r.m.s. Rangitiki* on the UK/ Panama Canal/New Zealand run, each trip lasting just short of four months.

On that first trip in 1957, as we made our way from Tilbury across the Atlantic Ocean towards our first port and refuelling station at Caracas Bay, Curacao, in the Netherland Antilles - a port at which a few years later I was hospitalised with appendicitis - we found ourselves on the outskirts of a full blown hurricane. We received an SOS distress message from a ship called *Pamir*, which had encountered difficulties and was about 400 miles from us. The *Pamir* was a famous ship known throughout the world, as she was the last commercially employed square rigged sailing ship, having an international crew that numbered 86.

The *Rangitiki* was a strong liner, built in the famous Harland and Wolff shipyards of Belfast in

1929, and she could handle the mountainous seas with comparative ease. In normal weather conditions we were only one day's steaming from the *Pamir*. But our very experienced captain, Commodore Lettington, who was then the senior captain in the fleet, decided he could not compromise the integrity of his command by risking his ship and passengers in such weather, and so we remained 'hove to', riding out the storm and not able to render assistance. This story had a sad ending, with not only the sinking of the world's last commercial sailing ship, but also with the loss of 80 of her crew - a most sobering lesson for a young 16 year old Midshipman!

r.m.s. **RANGITIKI**

Those early days at sea quickly merged into weeks, months and years, as I was totally and utterly immersed in living my dream. During those first five years of my sea-going career I managed to return home to New Zealand and see my parents on a regular basis. What a great life we had - we worked hard, we studied hard and, within the limits of a 'Middie's' meagre pay, we played as hard as we could too!

Usually the general cargo ships would carry four Midshipmen aboard during each voyage. We all lived somewhere amidships (hence the term Midshipmen), invariably in a cabin with no portholes or windows, and often with questionable ventilation. Air conditioning was unheard of in the 1950's and 1960's aboard British Merchant Ships.

PAMIR

Although we were generally well cared for, nevertheless we were treated by many Chief Officers as a cheap pair of hands to work on deck. We earned a pittance compared to the ship's sailors, alongside whom we worked and learned from. We also had to 'stand a watch' on the bridge, understudying the Officer of the Watch. On top of all that, we midshipmen were expected to study for our professional examinations, do our own washing, ironing and keep our accommodation up to scratch. There were not many hours left in the day for ourselves. Having worked as deck hands throughout most of the day, we then had to scrub up and present ourselves for inspection to check whether we were clean enough to join the officers for meals in the Officers' Mess. There we would all sit in general silence at our own table; it was a question in those days of being seen and not heard!

In spite of this, life at sea, at least for me, never seemed to be a hardship. There were always different ships to look at and I enjoyed the fellowship of my equally hard pressed 'would be' brother officers, and the encouragement given from those Deck Officers who were charged to teach us all they knew about a life at sea; and not least of all, those other things of which our mothers would not have approved; we were sailors after all!

Whatever my school teachers back home in New Zealand may have thought about my academic abilities, I was now always up there among the top three in the monthly study returns. This helped to boost my self-confidence as I realised that I could keep up with the other Midshipmen who had taken their schooling more seriously than I had. Although to start with, I was definitely behind my contemporaries academically, within a couple of years I had caught them up. Looking back, I am still amazed at how my ambitions helped me overcome a slow start.

At the beginning of the 1960's, when shipping companies were diversifying, P&O was no different. The Company, along with quite a few other 'traditional' shipping lines, started a programme of building oil tankers. It was during that cold wet December of 1960 when I found myself, along with three other Midshipmen, travelling from London to Glasgow by sleeper train, to join our first oil tanker anchored at the

'Tail of the Bank' on the River Clyde. All four of us only served for one round trip, but this was the maiden voyage of s.s. *Kent,* which, at 49,000 tons, was then one of the largest of all British oil tankers.

Sailing from Greenock we made our way down through stormy seas to the Suez Canal which we passed through on Christmas Day. Our destination was Mena-al-Ahmadi - the massive oil terminal in Kuwait. Because there were restrictions in draught of ships - that is to say, how much of the ship's hull is under the water - passing through the Suez Canal, we were forced to load only a part cargo of crude oil and then, on our way back to the UK we stopped off at Sidon, in the Lebanon, to top up.

s.s. **KENT**

Sidon was one of the great seaports of the Phoenicians and continued to be a port of great significance under the Persians within the Hellenistic world, and later in the Roman Empire.

Although I decided early on that trip that oil tankers were not my choice mode of going to sea, the long days and nights of being 'out there' on the vast wide oceans of the world was one part of going to sea which I most enjoyed. Crossing the Pacific from Panama to New Zealand and vice versa would take between sixteen and eighteen days, depending on the weather, without sight of any land or sighting many other ships. It was here that we all experienced the complete freedom of wide-open spaces and untainted pure fresh air. The downside to this was that, on arrival in an industrial port with its polluted air and contaminated waters, we were susceptible to the local bugs. When at sea, quite often, out on the vast open oceans, the only other company to be had were occasional accompanying dolphins swimming at the bow of our ship or a whale coming up for air. Whales may well be wonderful creatures, worthy of preservation, but if one 'blows' close to your ship and you happen to be 'downwind' of it; believe me that's when you start to fully understand the meaning of the term 'fishy smell'! When in the Southern Hemisphere we would marvel at the majesty of the great wandering albatross gliding effortlessly on the wind, thousands of miles from the nearest land.

Somewhat unexpectedly, and towards the end of my indentures, I was offered an appointment with another of P&O's subsidiary companies, Strick Line, as an unqualified ('un-certificated' was the actual word used in those days) Third Officer. "*Was I interested?*" I was asked. I mean to say, what a foolish question! Before I knew it, I had joined the 7,500 ton freighter *m.v. Tangistan* in the West India Docks and sailed from London, outbound to the Persian Gulf.

That single trip to the Persian Gulf and back to Continental Europe lasted just over four months, and by the time I had paid off (left) the ship, it was time to go back to nautical college. At long last, I had acquired the actual sea-time necessary, which allowed me to sit my first professional examination.

The first three days of any of the three staged professional examinations for ship's deck officers were taken up with six written papers, the pass mark of which was 70%. If this figure was not attained in the first paper, the examiner never even bothered looking at the others! This was followed by an old-fashioned 'Signals' examination, where the candidate had to prove his proficiency in both reading and sending of morse code, reading and sending of semaphore, as well as a full knowledge of the international code and etiquette of signal flags. Finally, one was faced with up to two hours of 'orals' - a viva examination whose pass grade, it seemed, depended a lot on the whims of the examiner.

m.v. TANGISTAN

The normal full-time study course at college ashore for a "2nd Mates Certificate of Competency" or "2nd Mates Ticket", as it was universally known, was three to four months, but I was in a hurry. I attended the King Edward VII Nautical College at the bottom of Commercial Road in the heart of London's East End and Docklands. Confident that I was God's answer to the British Merchant Navy, I presented myself for the examination after only 6 weeks, and surprised most people by passing first time.

But it was not 'all work and no play' during those college days, for we nautical students somehow happened to team up with the student nurses from the Queen Elizabeth 2nd Hospital for Children at Bethnal Green. By mutual consent our common local pub, although miles from both the nautical college and the children's hospital, was the Prospect of Whitby, down on the banks of the River Thames at Wapping. This pub was made famous by visits from HRH Princess Margaret and consorts, but we students liked to feel that we too had a hand in its popularity, and most certainly in the profits!

It seemed that nothing could stop me now. Here I was, newly qualified, with a brand new 2nd Mates ticket in my pocket. However, I did have the sense to realise that, although now qualified and having my foot on the first rung of the ladder, I was about to start my real education on how to be a successful ship's officer.

Chapter 3

The Ladder of Promotion

On receiving my 'Ticket', I immediately applied to join the main fleet of P&O and, having been accepted, I requested an immediate sea-going appointment. As a newly qualified navigating officer, P&O viewed me quite differently. No longer was I a Midshipman, so my name had the prefix of 'Mr' and, for now, being an officer entitled me to both courtesy and respect. So, Mr Wells was dispatched across to Antwerp to join a ship as her 3rd Officer. This was an 8,000 ton general freighter, *m.v. Surat*, which was at that time loading a full general cargo bound for Australia.

After that cargo was discharged we crossed the Tasman Sea empty and in ballast to New Zealand, where another full cargo was loaded, this time comprising mainly refrigerated foodstuffs for both European and UK ports.

m.v. SURAT

Can you imagine the excitement when, eight weeks after sailing from Antwerp, we docked in my home port of Wellington, where all of my family were waiting there on the quayside? My father's pride in me was almost tangible as we stood there hugging each other, much to the amusement of the on-looking crew. Proudly boasting one gold stripe on my arm, I am sure my family thought I was there to guide and advise the Captain and not the other way around!

One year's sea-time later and it was time to go back ashore, this time in Hull, to study for and successfully pass my next examination - the 1st Mates Ticket. 'Sea-time' was the actual time served aboard ship and did not include any home leave, so one year's sea-time would usually take fourteen to sixteen months.

In the 1960's, the P&O Shipping Company was divided into passenger and cargo ship divisions. Now qualified as 1st Mate, I was asked whether I would be interested in serving within the passenger ship division. This was long before the days of cruise ships, and all of our passenger ships were on liner trades from the UK to India, the Far East, Australasia as well as the 'round the world' service. Delighted that I had even been asked, I was curious to know why, when there seemed to be many more suitable candidates than me. The Head Office, in the form of the Marine Superintendent, simply said "*that he thought there might be a bright future for me on the passenger ships*". So without too much thought, I said "*yes*", as I was interested in anything that would advance my promotion!

However, P&O liked their passenger ships to 'wear' a Blue Ensign, as opposed to the old 'Red Duster', as the Red Ensign is known. This meant that the majority of the ship's deck officers were required to be active members of the Royal Navy Reserve. If I were to transfer across to the passenger division, then I would have to be prepared to join the RNR and undertake all the required extra training. If that's what was required, then, no problem!

The next training course I found myself attending was the Company's 'charm school' based at Southampton. It was here where young officers were supposedly taught the finer points of being a passenger ship's officer! The course was meant to last four weeks, but after only two, I was called away to join another freighter whose second officer had been rushed into hospital overnight. Not only did I not return to complete that course, but I never did find out whether they had given up on me, or if I was so good I didn't need further tuition. My suspicions are that it was probably the former!

Whilst my employers facilitated my entry into the RNR, there were a couple more 'relief' jobs sailing around the coasts of the UK and Europe, as the ship's regular officers left to go home on leave and, having been accepted by Their Lordships at the Admiralty for service in the Royal Navy Reserve, I soon found myself with two of my contemporaries from P&O undergoing some rigorous training at Whale Island, Portsmouth. This was followed by three weeks intensive naval navigational training.

m.v. GLOUCESTER

Unlike today's modern seafarer who joins a ship knowing the date that he/she will be relieved and then flown home, no matter where in the world they may be, in the 1950's and '60's we joined a ship, signing on for a maximum of two years. In some shipping companies the officers and crew really did complete two years away from home. In P&O, given that all their ships, including the freighters, were employed on the liner trades, that is to say regular routes, the time spent aboard was usually just for a round trip to wherever the voyage took you. On average, the majority of the trips were in the region of three to six months. Personally, the longest trip that I ever undertook was as Midshipman aboard *m.v. Gloucester*, which lasted sixteen months.

We had sailed from the UK bound for Australia on what was to be a normal five to six month trip, but whilst out on the Australian coast, our ship was sub-chartered. Four round trips from Australia and New Zealand to several Pacific Islands, and then onto the west coast of both the USA and Canada, made those unexpected extra months pass quickly. All the officers and crew accepted their fate with a simple shrug of the shoulders: c'est la vie. I cannot envisage many of our modern seamen being happy with such a system!

Going to sea in those days seems so far removed from seafaring today. Although we tried to be efficient in everything we did and the way our ships were run, there was always an easygoing relaxed manner in which things were done. One cannot deny that many of the conditions we accepted as 'normal' would not be acceptable today, because now we all have to take heed of those strange and most difficult of people, the Health and Safety man and his counterpart: the Risk Assessment man. They just did not exist during my early days at sea. It may well be much more comfortable going away to sea today, but is it as much fun as it was?

With today's modern refrigerated food and microwave ovens, the crew have fresh food daily. We loved it when our ship was fully loaded, lying deep in the water and was sailing through those long low swells sometimes found in mid tropical oceans. For it was not an uncommon sight to see the ship's cook wandering around the main deck at daybreak, with a basket in his hand, picking up the flying fish that had unintentionally landed on the deck - the officers were certainly assured of fresh fish for breakfast on those fruitful days!

Another source of fresh fish came from quite a different source - there was one captain in particular who always wrote in his standing orders to the Officer of the Watch on the ship's bridge, to look out for waterspouts. A waterspout is in fact a sea tornado. These are short-lived natural phenomena, lasting anything from just a few minutes to half an hour – a rapidly gyrating vortex descends down from the clouds and, when it makes contact with the sea surface, it starts to suck up a column of water. This column can vary anywhere between one metre to one hundred metres in diameter. As they are known to be rather dangerous to shipping, most ships steer well clear of them.

A WATERSPOUT IN PORT

Our captain, in his standing orders, instructed the Officer of the Watch to alter course and, provided that it was safe to do so, to approach the waterspout downwind, as close as he dare. Working on the basis of 'what goes up must come down', as the waterspout started to diminish in strength the water column and its contents gravitated back down to earth, to where our waiting ship received not only a free deck wash, but hopefully a liberal supply of writhing fish as well. We lived well in those days!

My next deep-sea appointment was on one of the large modern cargo liners trading between Northern Europe and the Indian sub-continent. It was during this trip that I witnessed an incident, as I sat on a public bus with my friend Peter, the ship's Radio Officer, which was to have a profound effect on my life and my life's philosophy.

Our ship was docked in the Indian city of Visakhapatnam and, having a weekend off, we both decided that we should go and explore the town with its famous temple high on a hill, overlooking the entire city and port. It was in this temple where deadly green mambas draped themselves around the holy shrines, but were kept subdued by the incense from the burning joss sticks. It never crossed our minds to wonder what might happen if the supply of joss sticks ran out, or worse still, if the flames had been extinguished as we passed these deadly reptiles, all within hand's reach.

As both the Radio Officer and I wanted to taste Indian life as the Indians knew it, we took a public bus from the dock gates towards the shrine. In the general melee and continual traffic jams, common in most large Indian towns, at one point our bus was forced to stop and wait for the road to clear. Peter nudged my elbow and told me to take a look out of the window. There were hordes of people milling around and spilling out onto the street, and the usual beggars were plying their trade. One beggar in particular was haranguing a chap who was eating some chapatti bread. The beggar wanted it, or at least some of it, but the diner wanted nothing to do with him, so a heated argument broke out. It was obvious that the impasse would have to be resolved before our bus could move on, and so it was, but not in a way anyone from our world could imagine.

From deep within his clothes the beggar produced a dagger and, without warning, thrust it deep into the chest of the man eating his chapatti, who fell to the ground writhing. Without further ado the beggar withdrew his dagger, wiped the blood from its blade onto the poor stabbed man's clothes, removed the blood soaked bread, started to eat it, and then moved away as though nothing had happened. As the man lay dying on the road, the thing that struck both of us was that not one of the onlookers offered him aid.

That harsh lesson has stayed with me throughout my life, and consequently I find that I have little patience with those who gratuitously waste food....especially noticeable on some of the cruise ships on which I have had the privilege to be aboard as Guest Speaker; but more of that later.

I was only on that ship for one trip because, on my return to the UK, I was appointed Navigator aboard the passenger liner *s.s. Himalaya.* This ship was then on a 'round the world' service, one voyage sailing eastwards, outwards through the Suez Canal, the next westwards, outwards through the Panama Canal. This was long before the time we had satellites and computers to do the navigating for us, but I was in seventh heaven! Talk about a square peg in a square hole this was it! Navigating a large passenger liner, or indeed any type of ship, around the world, in the days when we relied on a sextant and a clear sky to see those heavenly bodies from which we found our position, was not only what I had been trained to do, but what I loved doing.

Promotion came steadily and sea service, interspersed with the occasional shore leave at home with my new wife, made the long months of actual sea-time required before I could sit my final sea-going professional examination just fly by.

Before I went ashore to sit my Finals to become a Master Mariner, I was promoted to Chief Officer. Although not an unknown occurrence in lesser shipping companies, this was most definitely a rarity in companies like the P&O – as it was standard practise for every deck officer to hold the qualifications of the next rank above that in which he sailed. But sometimes needs, simply must, and this was one of those rare occasions when I found myself to be in the right place at the right time. My appointment this time was aboard a rather old and battered freighter, way past her 'sell by date'.

s.s. **HIMALAYA**

What a contrast in living; in fact what a marked contrast in going to sea to the relative comfort of passenger liners. I knew that I would be required to spend more time aboard such ships before I returned to the passenger liners in a more senior rank, and it was during this time I realised that I preferred going to sea in the comfort of passenger ships! I had always harboured a desire to join the Pilotage service, and it was after sailing on the *Ballarat* that I started making active enquiries.

m.v. **BALLARAT**

Having completed my first trip as Chief Officer, I returned to nautical college to study for and sit my final sea-going examination: Master F.G. (Foreign Going i.e. unlimited worldwide). It was during those three months ashore living in a bed-sit in Essex, while commuting every day to the college in London, which confirmed my view that a humdrum life of being a regular worker commuting to work each and every day was definitely not for me. On the 9th October 1967 having passed my 'Master's Ticket', I was now a fully-fledged Master Mariner.

Before the ink had dried on my 'Ticket', there I was back before the Marine Superintendent offering myself for further sea service. I don't suppose my wife was too amused, as the following week saw me join another ship of the Fleet as Chief Officer, aboard a relatively new refrigerated cargo liner bound for Australia.

There are two things every professional mariner fears most when out in the middle of the oceans. The first is fire. You really are very aware that you are out there on your own should a fire break out aboard your ship, and you have to gather and use all the resources available. In spite of the unlimited amount of water surrounding the ship, its use must be judicial at such times in order to maintain the ship's stability.

The second is major medical emergencies. A British registered ship having a compliment of less than one hundred persons on board was not required by law to carry a qualified medical practitioner. The 'Doc', more often than not, was the Chief Officer who administered day-to-day medicines, stitched up any bad cuts and administered the occasional penicillin jab to the errant sailor when needed! For the more serious cases, radio advice was always available from an international medical unit based in Rome, Italy.

In those days, it was not unknown for young medical practitioners from both Australia and New Zealand to 'work their passage' to the UK where they furthered their medical studies and careers. In return for a free passage they would relieve the Chief Officer of his duties as the 'Doc'.

One such trip particularly stands out in my memory. We had completed the loading of our cargo and were finally ready to sail from Australia non-stop back to Europe when our port agent brought on board a person purporting to be a qualified doctor. He stands out in my mind's eye as clearly today as he did all those years ago. I can only describe him as: young, hairy, scruffy, dirty and smelly. He was unlike any medical professional I had, or have ever since, met. Our captain, who was a typical P&O master from the 'old school' summoned me to his quarters and, with a complete look of disdain, instructed me to 'find "*it*" somewhere to sleep'.

We sailed from Sydney making our way south and then across the notorious Australian Bight and, as we ploughed through those very heavy swells inevitably encountered south of Australia, the ship's motion became rather excessive. I found myself holding clinics again as our doctor confined himself to bed having convinced himself that he was dying of seasickness. Whatever thoughts any of us might have harboured about our somewhat unsavoury passage worker were dispelled a few days later in the calmer waters of the Indian Ocean.

An engine-room crew member had been complaining of stomach pains and, after a couple of consultations, our doctor decided that he was suffering from acute appendicitis. We were at least five days steaming from the nearest port, so the doctor decided he would have to perform an operation to remove the offending appendage. The night before the operation our 'doc' spent most of the evening in his cabin with his head buried deep into his medical books. Such was the esteem in which he was held that one of our junior officers suggested he was probably reading something like "Teach Yourself Surgery". As he could not manage the operation alone, it fell on me to be the 'surgeon's' assistant. I don't know who was more nervous, the doctor or me, but with the ship hove to and heading directly into the swell to minimise the motion and, both of us having 'scrubbed up' and now fully gowned, we were ready.

I don't remember much of the operation itself except that there was a lot of blood and the doctor spent most of the time huffing and puffing as well as swearing and cursing. Afterwards he confessed he had never done anything like that before and was quite proud of himself that his patient actually survived! No one knew quite what to say to that and for the remainder of the voyage our doctor, having finally found his sea-legs, strutted around the decks as any proud peacock might. He never really fitted into the Officer's Wardroom on a P&O cargo liner and when an unexpected opportunity to leave the ship at Gibraltar was provided, he took it without hesitation.

Whilst on the subject of survival at sea, back in the 1950's and 1960's, all sea-going passengers were subject to a clause in the 'conditions of carriage' - to be found on the back of their travel ticket - that if death occurred whilst at sea and the ship was more than forty eight hours from the next scheduled arrival port, then the body would have to be buried at sea. The simple reason for this was insufficient refrigerated space on board where a body could be stored.

On my second voyage to sea aboard the *Rangitiki* somewhere out in the Pacific Ocean one of our passengers suffered a heart attack and was certified dead by the ship's doctor. After the next of kin had said their goodbyes and the medical department had prepared the body, it was then handed over to the deck department. The Chief Officer thought it would be 'character building' if the two young Midshipmen were present to witness the final preparation of a body for burial at sea. Iron fire bars were brought from somewhere deep within the ship's engine room and placed between the legs and below the knees of the deceased. This ensured two things: 1. the body would enter the water feet first, as was required by tradition, and 2. it would immediately sink.

Can you imagine the trauma, for a number of the passengers as they leaned across the ship's rails watching proceedings, to say nothing for the next of kin, as the body of their loved one slowly refloated in front of their very eyes and wallowed in the swell and a boat then had to be lowered to retrieve it and try all over again? Another tradition that was religiously observed from the days of yore was when the Bosun's

Mate was sewing the canvas around the body, he had to ensure that the last stitch actually pierced the deceased nostrils. This confirmed the body was in fact dead. Our body was, and I have often wondered since, what would be the reaction of the burial team if, when piercing the nostrils, the body gave an almighty leap and shout...! Anyway, with prayers led by our captain, buried at sea he was, immediately sink he did, our ensign was raised from 'half mast', and we resumed on our way increasing to full speed. Another day at sea!

Eight happy months later - that was two 'round' voyages - saw me once again in front of the 'boss' back at HQ in London. The Marine Superintendent was a wonderful reader of his officers and his assessment of me was no different. He knew how ambitious I was, and in fact he had, without my being aware, nurtured my career ever since I joined the Fleet with that brand new single stripe on my uniform. I learnt some years later that he even had an inkling of my Pilotage aspirations.

The meeting was opened without preamble: "*Wells*" he said "*I have been watching your progress up the ladder for some years now, and cannot help but admire your single mindedness and dedication. Now I know there are many of your brother officers who will think you are not yet ready, but I feel, given the right opportunity, you'll do a good job. But the really important question is whether YOU think you are ready to take command?*" I could not believe what I was hearing. I mean what a totally stupid question to ask someone like me! "*Yes Sir*", I responded, without giving it a moment's thought -"*where and when do I join the ship?*"

Having committed myself, Capt. Yardley then told me the bad news. P&O were offering, with the support of the British Government, to provide the Federal Government of Nigeria with a supply of senior officers and masters for their newly formed shipping line. My command was not with P&O as I had anticipated, but on secondment to the Nigerian National Shipping Line. Still, I reckoned I could cope with that. However, what I had overlooked was, at that particular time in history, Nigeria was being torn asunder by a very bloody civil war: the Biafran War.

Having signed the agreement to be seconded there and then in the Superintendent's office, and having agreed to a period of secondment for two years, I floated home to our house in Essex where I ecstatically informed my 'not too amused wife' that, having only just attained my 28th birthday, I was now a Captain and going off to a war zone. I ignored her pleas and reminders that I was also a father and had other responsibilities. Today perhaps, I imagine that I could empathise with her point of view more easily, simply because I am older and hopefully a lot wiser. I can now see the 'wider' picture, appreciating that there is more to life than pursuing one's career.

With the papers signed and witnessed, it was now too late to have a change of heart, not that such a thought ever entered my mind, as I was literally too excited. Later I learned the same offer had been made to other chief officers within the Fleet, who were senior to and more experienced than me, but they had all turned it down. Perhaps, just perhaps, I should not have been so eager. Who knows? Such opportunities are very few and far between and, when one came my way, I grabbed it with both hands.

Within a week I received my uniforms back from the naval tailors proudly sporting four gold stripes, plus a new cap covered in 'scrambled egg'. So I was ready. Again, little did I know just what I was letting myself in for.

Chapter 4

Command

The trips from Northern Europe to Nigeria and back usually lasted about six weeks. For my first trip on secondment, I was aboard a ship with the wonderful name of *m.v. Oba Ovonramwen* as Staff Captain, a rank created for that particular trip, as I understudied an experienced captain.

m.v. OBA OVONRAMWEN

Two weeks into the trip and fully loaded down to our Marks (the Plimsoll Line) we entered the darkness of Freetown harbour in Sierra Leone. Disaster struck as we hit Carpenter's Rock and became stuck fast. The first I knew of this was when I was called from my bed, informed we were aground, and told that my presence on the bridge was required immediately.

Carpenter's Rock lies to the south of the accredited track into the open harbour of Freetown, where a strong cross-current ebbs and flows with the tide, and has, over the years, had its fair share of unfortunate visitors. Ribs, frames and other bits and pieces of wreckage from ships that had met their end on the rock, were clearly visible at low water. Unfortunately for us, we ran aground when we were still fully loaded, consequently we were lying deep in the water and it was just before the high tide. The tide, when it turned, also turned our ship and we settled down onto the rising steel frames of former victims. As the tide fell away, so we settled lower and lower onto the reef, and those upright steel frames punctured our ship's bottom, which in turn allowed sea-water to flood the drinking water tanks.

Daylight came out of the east (as it always does in Africa, with undue haste) then in the cold light of day, we could now get a better assessment of our situation. It was not good, and I could only thank my lucky stars that I was nowhere near the bridge when we struck!

We sat on that reef for six weeks, whilst cargo was jettisoned over the side in order to lighten the ship, so that at the next highest tide attempts to refloat her could be made. It was sad to see perfectly good cargo literally being dumped over the side, especially so, as this included a brand new Rolls Royce destined for the British Ambassador to Ghana!

The stories which could be told about those six and the following four weeks would fill volumes. There was rampant pilfering by locals who, as they watched the cargo of foodstuff being dumped over the side, decided this was too good an opportunity for them to miss feeding their impoverished families. They boarded our wrecked ship in droves, helping themselves to whatever they wanted. This sort of situation highlights the stupidity of many of the laws we are obliged to live by. Personally, I could see no reason for not offering the local population the foodstuff we had to jettison. After all it was going to waste and would only be food for the marine life living in those local waters. Think of the good local goodwill it would have afforded us.

But no, that was too simple, because the insurance underwriters insisted that all the cargo, including foodstuff, be jettisoned over the ship's side. This in turn created major headaches for us on board because of the aggressiveness and willingness to use physical violence exhibited by those locals who had boarded our ship. Eventually, units of the local militia came aboard to control and repel the invaders. But this was West Africa, and they too were badly paid, hungry and had their own families ashore to feed...and so all that happened was that we officers and crew slept safely at night, as the foodstuffs were now being redirected towards the militia and their families.

This was the first, and only, time that I have ever had to sleep with an armed guard squatting outside my cabin door for protection, but it did not stop chicken legs and feathers from being hung over the entrance to my quarters - a supposed jinx imposed on the occupier after a visit to or by the local witch doctor or medicine man as he is known today.

Because we had no fresh water aboard - it had all been contaminated by sea-water when the ship's bottom tanks were ruptured - both the officers and crew cleaned their teeth in Chivas Regal (honestly!). Fortunately the rains had come to West Africa, so we luxuriated by having rainwater showers out on deck. We had long passed worrying about modesty and were intent on grabbing what simple pleasures we could.

Generally speaking, everything was pretty much a shambles and there was almost nothing any of us could do. Some of the cargo was being discharged from the ship into barges, ranging up and down the ships side in the moderate to heavy swells that were running. The combination of several tons of free-swinging cargo being lowered into barges, which in turn were being subjected to uncontrolled movement caused by the swell, created a cocktail of extreme danger to the dock labourers working in the barges. A total of four local stevedores were crushed and killed by this heavy swinging cargo, and a further one was drowned whilst helping himself to cargo from parts of the ship which were awash.

One evening, when the roll call of dock labour about to go ashore showed one man missing, a search was carried out by both stevedore supervisors and ship's personnel. Eventually, down in cargo hold number four, where foodstuffs had been loaded on top of bagged cement, there, floating in the filthy flooded waters, in between the frames or ribs of the ship, he was found. The top of his head was about six feet below the top of the cement cargo which, by now, was waterlogged and one solid block. He was obviously dead and literally beyond the reach of any of us. The captain, chief officer and I, accompanied by the ship's bosun (the ship's foreman), descended into the cargo hold to review the situation.

The cargo could not be moved, and so we were faced with the problem of how to get him out. It would have been both an impossible and unacceptable risk to send even our smallest crew member down between the frames, so we adjourned back up top to our accommodation, where a conference of all the ship's officers and senior petty officers was called. Chaired by the captain, everybody was invited to throw in his suggestions. We had very few choices, so finally there was only one solution - we would have to lower a rope noose, lasso the body and physically haul him up.

Back down into the darkened cargo hold we went, carrying a length of good stout rope. Nobody, but nobody, wanted the job of lassoing the dead dockworker, so it became a question of pulling rank and the bosun caught the short straw. After several attempts, finally the loop caught around the semi-rigid arm and we all pulled in concert to heave the body vertically up a six-foot wall of cargo, and then laid him out on top of the hardened cement for a detailed examination. By now the authorities were aboard - Chief of Police and his men, a representative from the local coroner's office, Customs and Immigration, ship's agent, and even a member from the local press, most of whom came only for the free drinks and cigarettes. Not only were these free handouts deemed politically correct, but they also oiled many of the bureaucratic wheels within local port authorities. Known throughout the shipping world as OCS, translating into 'On Company Service', this service was, generally speaking, considered a 'bribe', but one well worth paying. The *m.v. Oba Ovonramwen*, her fate, and all the escapades on board, was hot local news!

After the body had been minutely examined and everyone from the shore had had their say, it was taken away pending an official inquiry. The captain and I retired to his quarters where we opened, and consumed, a full bottle of brandy and, in the circumstances, neither one of us was even mildly affected by its contents.

The ship's Master, Captain Jack Hogg from Scotland, was not only my mentor from whom I learned a great deal – especially, about how to act when under the utmost pressure - but we also became good friends. His untimely death from a cerebral haemorrhage was brought on it was believed, by the stresses and pressures he was subjected to in the aftermath of this incident and by the loss of his command.

It is surprising how adversity brings about feelings of camaraderie, a depth of feeling I had never before, or since, shared in all the years I have been at sea. Rank and uniforms went 'out of the window' as every man and boy aboard ignored the usual departmental rivalries and pulled his weight, putting in more hours of physical hard labour than ordinarily would have been expected from them.

Our labours were directed by the Salvage Master, an employee of the Dutch salvage experts, Smits of Rotterdam. They had been offered by the Nigerian Government a "Lloyds Open Form". This is an internationally accepted salvage contract based on "No Cure, No Pay". It was very much therefore in the salvor's interest to "cure" the problem and to do so in the shortest time possible.

In addition to the crew sent out by Smits for the actual salvage, as one could probably expect, every man and his dog flew to Freetown, mainly from London to give their 'expert' advice: salvors, surveyors, representative from the owners, representatives from the P & I Clubs, that is to say both the ship's and cargo insurers, plus a few others who, it appeared, came only for the ride and perhaps the OCS.

Our ship was an 'old lady' who had seen and provided many years of good service. Finally, after she had been refloated and towed into Freeport harbour, the divers had the chance to examine her bottom. Sadly, because no mariner of whatever persuasion likes to see a ship die, even after all the concerted efforts put in by everyone, it was concluded that the costs involved to salvage and repair her outweighed her actual value. She was therefore declared "CTL" - Constructive Total Loss and condemned to the scrap yard.

Ten action-packed weeks after attempting to enter Freetown, all the officers and crew left the ship.

She was in a very sad state: rusty, listing, leaking and dying. She was eventually sold for scrap and ended her life, as many crack liners and other ships have done, in one of the demolition yards somewhere along the Indian Coast.

During the three weeks of very welcome home leave that followed, I got to know a little chap who was now not only walking but starting to talk as well, and who was bemused that this strange man had come to live in his house. I am not sure to this day whether he really knew then that I was his father!

The day finally came when orders arrived through for me to fly to Lagos, where I would take command of a fine 12,000 ton cargo ship with accommodation for twelve passengers: *m.v. Ahmadu Bello*, named after a Nigerian chieftain.

Lagos was in many ways an interesting city, sitting as it does on the eastern side of the Lagos Lagoon. On the western side of the lagoon was the new port of Apapa, built on an island known as Tin Can Island. This was the original site of Lagos' city rubbish dump, and both ports were just a couple of miles from the open ocean. When I was there in the latter part of the 1960's, Lagos was the capital city of Nigeria and, between 1820 and 1875, this place was notorious for being one of the main centres for the West African Slave Trade. In February 1976, the foundations for a completely new city, that was destined to become Nigeria's new capital city, were laid. This city was to be built out in the open bush and, almost sixteen years later, Nigeria's capital was moved from Lagos to the new city of Abuja.

In those days I travelled on my New Zealand passport in addition to my seaman's papers, and while these usually granted me unhindered passage, many Third World Governments and their overseas embassies had so much bureaucracy, that even a simple granting of a visa often became an extremely complicated matter. Bureaucracy being what it was, inevitable delays were experienced in obtaining my visa, and so I missed my scheduled evening's flight down to Lagos.

m.v. AHMADU BELLO

It was in the late 1960's when Nigerian Airways had chartered one BOAC VC10, which flew from London to Lagos via Rome and Kano, every other day. God, my guardian angel, my lucky stars - call it what you will - was certainly looking out for me. To this day I remain convinced that the delay was 'ordained' because as the flight took off from Kano in Northern Nigeria for the last leg of its flight, a rebel's bomb hidden in the cargo department was detonated, resulting in total loss of the plane and all on board. This was a most sobering moment, not only for my immediate family, but for me as well and, perhaps, a harbinger of what awaited me as I flew two nights later into what was an internationally recognised war zone.

Lagos was relatively quiet as we travelled the dozen or so miles south from the airport at Ikeja into town and then on to the Port. But clearly a vicious inter-tribal war, chronic crime problems, religious intolerances, overcrowding in poor living conditions and the breakdown of ordinary life was pushing the country to its extreme limits. And there, in the capital city of Nigeria, no matter where one looked, all that was to be seen were derelict buildings and abject poverty. It was so sad to see such a decline from the glory days of Nigerian prosperity, just a few years earlier.

As we approached Lagos Port, I eagerly and excitedly scanned the various funnels of those ships docked there, seeking out the familiar large white N on a green and black funnel. And there she was, her silhouette proudly standing tall from the other surrounding ships - my first command!

I was greeted at the gangway by a junior officer and led up to the Captain's quarters. There I met a tired looking elderly gentleman whose first words were: "*Thank God you're here, I can't wait to get away*". Not an encouraging start, but when I learned he had suffered a mild stroke a few days earlier, I started to understand why he was so pleased to see me.

One thing I came to understand, and reluctantly had to accept, during the period I was seconded to the National Nigerian Shipping Line, was that no matter what needed doing, it would be done in African time. The word *WAWA*, with a resigned shrug of the shoulders, soon became all too familiar: West Africa Wins Again! No man, and certainly no white man, was ever going to change this frustratingly laid back attitude.

Years later, when living with my family in both the Middle East and the Bahamas, I would often smile to myself and silently mouth the word *WAWA*, substituting whichever country I was in at that time for "West Africa".

One upshot of this frame of mind is that, in all the years I have lived and worked in Africa, the Middle East and the Bahamas, I have never encountered a local who suffered from ulcers, stress, high blood pressure or heart problems!

All too soon it was time for us to sail for Northern Europe and, with the pilot aboard and the ship all ready, I proudly gave the order to "*let go fore and aft*" and we were away. This remains one of the defining moments of my professional life - sailing out of port on a long ocean passage and bearing the ultimate responsibility as Master of all I surveyed.

Although my learning curve was pretty much vertical, I enjoyed those first days of having the ultimate command and responsibility, not only for my ship, but for her cargo and the lives of my officers, crew and passengers as well. I was fortunate in that I had a good efficient crew and reasonably competent officers. On those rare occasions when called to the bridge in a rush, I was glad that my training was so comprehensively thorough with both P & O and the Royal Navy Reserve, enabling me to confidently handle whatever situation arose. In many ways we were perhaps a lucky ship for, despite the front line action we saw and experienced in the coming months, we all came through unscathed.

What we did see, and what became a nightly occurrence during the blackout of Lagos and its ports, was what we referred to as "bonfire night". Each night when we were in port, my officers and I, having had dinner, retired to the boat deck to relax under an awning where we were served drinks. Almost on the stroke of 8pm most nights, the low roar of an old Douglas Dakota DC3 aircraft could be heard flying in from the east.

How he ever became involved no one really knew, but there was a Swedish Count who had become a mercenary pilot and was flying on behalf of Biafra. Unofficial word had it that he had been cashiered out of the Scandinavian civil airline SAS, for more than one occasion having had 'one too many' before flying. Anyway, each night, there he was - flying in low and slow through the blackout darkness over Lagos, starting at the seaward end of the lagoon. When they remembered, or could be bothered, inefficient and half-hearted rifle fire was returned by those soldiers on the ground that happened to have live ammunition to hand!

The Count always flew the plane solo. On the right hand seat of the cockpit he stored boxes of hand grenades and, at regular intervals, he would take one, extract the pin with his teeth, then count off the necessary seconds before simply throwing it out of the plane's window. More often than not the grenade exploded harmlessly in the air or into the water.

But one dark and stormy night, when we were all sitting up on deck, waiting expectantly for the fireworks to start, sure enough the familiar drone of his two engines was heard over the rising howl of the wind. A couple of runs up and down the lagoon passed off uneventfully with the regular 'grump' of an exploding hand grenade. Then, on his third run, (and here one can only assume) he picked up a grenade and pulled the pin at the very same time that the plane took a sudden sheer in the wind. One must conclude that the grenade was dropped and rolled under his seat...! The explosion as the DC3 blew up was the most spectacular we had seen throughout all the time I was in the war zone. We missed the mad Swedish Count after that; our evening entertainment whilst in Lagos lagoon was never quite the same.

One January day, when lying quietly discharging our cargo in the port of Apapa just across the lagoon from Lagos, I received word that the Biafran leader Ojukwu had capitulated and the war was effectively over. As a Nigerian ship, we were ordered by the government to stop all discharge of our cargo and prepare to take aboard members of the Federal armed forces, as well as various types of equipment, and sail for Port Harcourt the former 'garden city' of Nigeria. Port Harcourt lay on the banks of the swift flowing Bonny River, about 20 miles inland; a delta in the vast River Niger.

To everyone's amazement, several army trucks were seen to pull up alongside our ship, where, with powerful hoses, they were washed clean. When dried, they were painted white with the words stencilled in red on the doors "A Gift from the People of Great Britain". Somehow I cannot help but suspect that the monies from Great Britain for new trucks disappeared into various pockets, whilst some enterprising person just happened to find some old army trucks. *WAWA!*

They were finally loaded aboard and, as soon as we could, we set off for the 24-hour passage across to 'PH', as Port Harcourt was affectionately known.

The last time I had been in PH was the morning it fell once again to the Rebels. PH was one of those pivotal cities in the Biafran war, as it often alternated between being occupied by either the Federal Troops or the Rebels. We were waiting in the port of PH, all ready to sail, but we could not sail until daylight, as all navigational marks in the river had been removed and it was far too dangerous to try and attempt a river passage in the dark. Little sleep was had by anybody that night as the sky was lit up with gun flashes - we knew that the rebel troops were rapidly closing, as the sound of heavy gunfire boomed and the rattle of light arms grew ever closer. As dawn gathered, I was becoming ever more concerned for my ship and crew. As soon as we had sufficient daylight and could see across to the riverbank on the other side, we cut our ropes and sailed away. It was around 7am and PH fell about two hours later, far too close a call for my comfort.

However, going back to that trip when we transported those gifts from the British people...we had an uneventful passage from Apapa and, as soon as we docked in PH, the army personnel disembarked and then the discharge of those vehicles began. All was going smoothly until the General in command of the *illustrious victorious 3rd core commando unit* – the actual name given to the unit - invited himself into my quarters not only to drink my Scotch, but also to inform me that I had a priority passage back to Lagos as a mercy ship. We were to transport over 3000 wounded men, ranging from those near to death to the walking wounded.

At first this did not unduly concern me, as we would rig up awnings on the decks for the men, and after all it was only a 24-hour run back in ideal sailing conditions. What I was not told was that there would be only a handful of non-commissioned officers (sergeants and corporals), NCO's, from the army who would be in charge of these men. The other thing they somehow conveniently forgot to tell me until the very last moment was that there would be no medical orderlies or medical supplies, no food and, most importantly, no water provided. Now this did present us with a problem, because we only had minimum provisions and water on board for the ship's officers and crew. So, whilst wounded soldiers were being brought aboard and settling themselves down for the passage back to Lagos, an emergency meeting was convened on board my ship between the General in command, his staff, me, my senior officers and engineers. The one overriding priority was to have the ship's crew fully functional, that is to say 'fed and watered', in order that we could operate the ship efficiently and maintain safety. It was an extremely difficult decision to reach, and regrettably we had no alternative but to refuse all requests for any form of sustenance from our unexpected passengers.

What a terrible decision for anybody, let alone a 29 year old to have to make; when men who were obviously dying and begging for a little water, we had to harden our hearts and say no. But if we had given to one where would it have stopped? Unfortunately, four soldiers died from their wounds en-route to Lagos

With a full complement of officers and crew, over 3000 wounded battle-hardened troops and only 12 NCOs, we finally left PH and made our way back to Lagos at maximum speed. We made it back in less than 24 hours, and were given priority clearance to enter port to proceed directly to a special berth where ambulances were waiting to take the badly injured to hospital.

Yes, later on, I did have nightmares over that return trip to Lagos, but what really bothered me most of all was what could have happened. How would we have coped, if those less wounded had decided to take it into their heads to help themselves to the ship's provisions? With just 12 NCOs armed only with swagger sticks, there would have been very little they, or the ship's crew could have done. It was then I discovered that like everybody else who achieves the highest ranks in life - no matter what field – all are forced by their very positions to accept the responsibility of making some unpopular and difficult decisions. And that was one of the hardest I have ever had to make.

I have often been asked whether the time I spent in Nigeria was dangerous and were my ship and crew ever in any real danger. The answer is definitely 'yes' to both questions, and on several occasions. I don't like to dwell on what might have happened and therefore there is no point in worrying about what might have been! Was it all worth it? Well, I would have never been given my command in a regular British shipping line at the age I received mine, so professionally speaking, yes, it was.

Now the Biafran war was over, life on the West Coast of Africa – Nigeria, in particular, did not improve. Having achieved the rank and being confirmed as Master (the first year in command was always on a probationary basis), I decided that now I was on the top sea-going rung of the ladder, it was time to look further ahead in my sea-faring career. I knew that when or even if my parent company took me back, then I would be the youngest Captain in the fleet. I could also understand any number of the senior chief officers, who perhaps had refused an early command with the Nigerian National Shipping Line, would without a doubt object strongly. Deep within, if I was honest with myself, I couldn't really blame them either. It was then that I actively sought an opening in the Pilotage service; any port, anywhere.

Chapter 5

Entering the Pilotage Service

As I have indicated earlier, unbeknown to me, it had been an open secret with my main employers, the P&O Line, that my real ambition lay in becoming a pilot; although I was not unduly worried which port or in which country that would be, provided it had a busy harbour. The first to offer me an appointment would be the one I would accept. As luck would have it, I was invited to present myself before the esteemed body of the Elder Brethren of Trinity House, to explain why I thought I was the best candidate, and why I should be offered the forthcoming single appointment as a River Pilot in the Port of London. That was not an interview for the self-effacing or faint hearted! The term 'Pilotage District' is given to a particular stretch or area of water, estuary, river or harbour and port in which a pilot is licensed to operate. Things must have gone well for me, because out of the 65 candidates, guess who was the lucky one? I then went 'on the list' and all I had to do was wait to be 'called'.

A few months later the call came, and after resigning my command with the Nigerian Federal Government and P&O, I found myself now based at Gravesend, Kent, where the main pilot station for the Port of London is situated. From my very first day on station, I embarked on what was to become three and a half months of the most extremely concentrated hard work I have ever undertaken.

There is a general misconception that Trinity House Pilots were employed by Trinity House. They never were. All the pilots licensed by the 'House' were self-employed in the pilot district in which they operated, and answerable only to the ship's Master and ultimately the 'House' itself.

The rules were quite simple. Each qualifying pilot, who was known as a 'candidate' i.e. a pilot not yet licensed, had to undertake not less than three, nor more than six, months 'tripping' with other pilots before he could present himself before the Board for examination. A candidate 'trips' when he accompanies and observes another pilot who is both experienced and licensed. Occasionally, if he were lucky, the candidate would be allowed to perform an 'act of Pilotage', but whilst under strict supervision.

ABOUT TO PASS THROUGH TOWER BRIDGE

When first faced with the syllabus for the examination of my new district, the London River - that was from Gravesend in the East to London Bridge in the West, it would have been easy to become discouraged. Apart from the 24 nautical miles of winding tidal river, there were also 426 different berths, numerous buoy moorings, and other jetties up the creeks off the main river, in addition to the 8 dock complexes and locking-in systems. Not only did you have to know where each one was, but you also had to know the minimum amount of water on each of them at low tide as well as its length and maximum size ship that could be safely berthed there.

Additionally, one must have performed, under the guidance of a senior and experienced pilot, a minimum of 24 transits of Tower Bridge, 12 during the day, 12 during the night, 12 frontwards and 12 backwards.

After three and a half months of 'tripping', I was called before the Board, which it has to be said, was not the most welcoming. The expectation was that if you want a licence to pilot ships into and out of any harbour or port, then you must be capable of facing and holding your own in any environment, including a slightly hostile interrogation. I suppose it works, because years later, when I was an examining pilot sitting with the Elder Brethren of Trinity House, I took a similar line.

The examination was a 'viva voce', which could last for anything up to two hours depending on how confident the candidate was. The outcome included results of those various reports and assessments, recorded by other pilots with whom he had tripped. And the pass mark was a non-negotiable 98%. If the candidate failed to reach that figure he was automatically given a further two months 'tripping' before having to re-sit his examination for the second and final time. If he failed to reach that magic figure of 98% the second time around then that was that - he was finished with the Pilotage service before he had even begun. Amazingly, all of this time, that is to say - the three to eight months, was without pay! Who, in today's modern world, would be allowed to exercise such a system?

To those who do not understand this may well sound draconian, but every commercial marine pilot must know the waters in which he is licensed to operate like the back of his hand. As a passenger, would you feel comfortable if the pilot of your ship only had a rough idea of what he was doing or where he was? I think not!

The possibility of spending a maximum of eight months 'tripping' and then failing one's second examination had, believe me, quite an effect of focusing one's mind! Throughout the three and a half months I was subjected to that regime, my long-suffering wife stoically supported the family, not only financially, but also juggling her responsibilities as a wife, mother and school teacher.

As the strong tides swirl around the many bends of the River Thames, the soft mud bottom is naturally dredged. This means that on one side of the river it is not uncommon to find very deep water, whilst on the other side it is relatively shallow. This shouldn't present too much of a problem, except that at sea, on inland waters and navigable rivers, we drive on the right. So when two ships are approaching each other on a sharp bend, in order to 'hunt the deep water' it stands to reason that one must, at times, 'drive' on the wrong side of the river...! Unlike the amateur sailor when sailing his or her yacht up and down commercial rivers - who likes to keep right in the middle because that is where they think the deep water is - the professional pilot with his detailed and intimate knowledge of the waters is far less concerned with the deeper water than he is with the shallows. Working on the basis of 'worst case scenario', by knowing where the least amount of water is, we know where we can't go, and therefore we know where it is safe to go – now at first glance that may sound a bit like double-dutch, but it works very well in practice.

When first licensed, all pilots start off being classified as 'under draught', and that simply means that they are restricted to small ships of a certain size. As a pilot gains knowledge, experience, skill and confidence, he faces furthers examinations, and he works his way up the ladder to where he can start handling larger, and more importantly, deeper and consequently heavier ships. Eventually, pilots are cleared to operate ships of any size and draught anywhere within the designated District. It is at this stage that they are classified as Class 1 or Top Line pilots. In London's River District, it took a minimum of two years to become Class 1, during which time the pilot had opportunity to observe not only how the weather, but how the four seasons of the year, caused changes in the ebb and flow of the river.

It is interesting to note the confusion of many who are interested in, but not really knowledgeable about, the more technical side of ships. One looks at these huge cruise liners and considers them to be 'very big'. And big they are - there is no disputing that fact - but they are not 'heavy' ships.

Professional ship handlers are more concerned about the weight of the ship rather than its physical size. For example, Cunard's *Queen Mary 2*, when she first went into service, was described as the 'world's largest cruise ship' at around 150,000 tons. That particular tonnage is known as her Gross Registered Tonnage (GRT) which is, in fact, a volumetric measurement bearing no relation to the actual weight of the ship. One gross ton equals 100 cubic feet of certain enclosed spaces. The *QM2* has therefore, 150,000 x 100 = 15,000,000 (15 million) cubic feet of enclosed space; hence her gross tonnage. But, if she were to be lifted out of the water when fully loaded with passengers, stores and fuel, she would weigh somewhere in the region of 75,000 tons. Now, compare this with the world's largest commercial ship ever built, the *Jahre Viking* - an oil tanker whose gross tonnage measured 214,750 tons, but when fully laden with her cargo of oil, stores etc. weighed in at just over 825,000 tons. Although the gross tonnage difference between the two ships is 64,750 the actual or real weight difference is 750,000 tons. A very big difference, you'll agree.

It doesn't take much imagination to realise that both of these ships, although classed as 'big ships' (and neither having any brakes!) will handle in completely different ways. It should, by now, be obvious why the professional ship handler is so concerned with the weight of the ship, rather than consideration of her physical size.

S.S. JAHRE VIKING

After two full years piloting in London, and having risen to the dizzy heights of a Class 1 pilot, I found myself in that awkward position where our family mortgage was greater than my income. Oh dear, had my earning capacity suddenly come to a grinding halt? Back in the bad old days, when militant trade unionism ruled the roost in the British Docklands, all who were associated with the ports, directly or indirectly, were affected by the union's actions; not least self-employed Trinity House licensed pilots. During the early 1970's, ship owners were diverting the majority of their ships from the Port of London. With the number of ships calling into London drying up, this simply translated to self-employed pilots as: much less pay! Although there was, and still is to this day, little love lost between professional seafarers and ship owners, one could actually see the ship owners' point of view, as they diverted their ships from the UK ports to the more efficiently run and union free ports such as Antwerp, Rotterdam and Hamburg.

After a lot of heart searching, the older and possibly wiser pilots suggested that, whilst they remain piloting in London, the younger pilots could take sabbaticals and, if they still wished, return to London every 12 months and undertake the requisite 24 'acts of Pilotage' necessary to maintain their London Pilotage Licence – an opportunity no overly ambitious young pilot could ignore; particularly those with mortgages to pay! Having had to run such a gauntlet to get a pilot's licence, no one considered giving it up easily.

Within only a few weeks of my wife and I having discussed the situation and explored the options that were now open to us, we made the decision that I would apply for one of the marine vacancies with the National Iranian Oil Company. Having applied and been interviewed in London, about two months later a letter arrived offering me employment at their oil terminals in the Persian Gulf.

We arranged to rent out our home and my wife took the boys to her parents, whilst I flew to Abadan for the first of five overseas postings. This triggered the beginnings of a 14-year love affair as an expatriate pilot, known in the business as 'rent a pilot'.

Chapter 6
Iran

My first posting overseas was not as pilot but as a Tug Captain in the fascinating country of Iran, formerly known as Persia. I left for Iran alone and spent the first three weeks living in the Abadan International Hotel whilst the Oil Company tried to find suitable accommodation. My wife and two sons flew out to Iran six weeks after I had arrived there. We lived in a semi-detached house in the suburb of Bream which sat under the shadow of the oil refinery – then the largest in the world - and within easy view and walking distance of the Shatt el Arab River which marked the border with neighbouring Iraq.

Although we lived in Abadan, I worked first of all in the port of Bandar Mashar, sixty miles across the desert and salt flats of Khuzestan, and then latterly in the giant oil terminal on Kharg Island, a former penal colony out in the middle of the northern Persian Gulf. In both of these ports, all the tug masters were expatriates; many like me were in fact licensed pilots, others were tug captains from various British ports.

When working at Kharg Island we would fly to and from Abadan airport, working a 24 hour on and 48 hour off 'watch' basis. The Oil Company had its own fleet of aircraft, mostly operated by Dutch pilots on secondment from the Dutch national airline KLM. It was not really all that satisfactory, but it had to do pro tem.

We spent just under two years in Iran and, in many ways our lives were a series of contradictions. Our eldest son, aged 5, had started at the International school in Abadan, and my wife struggled with our other son only 2 years old - while trying to normalise both young lives in a new expatriate environment. Although

I was often away overnight she said that she never, at any time, felt unsafe in this foreign land.

After about six months living in Abadan, we decided that it was time to spread our wings a little and so we bought a car, a Peykan, which was an Iranian built Hillman Hunter. The boys would be loaded in the back, and we would wait for daybreak and then drive across the old Mesopotamia flatlands to Ahwaz, an oil company town built in the foothills of the Zagros mountain range. We would leave very early in order to get across the desert before the sun had

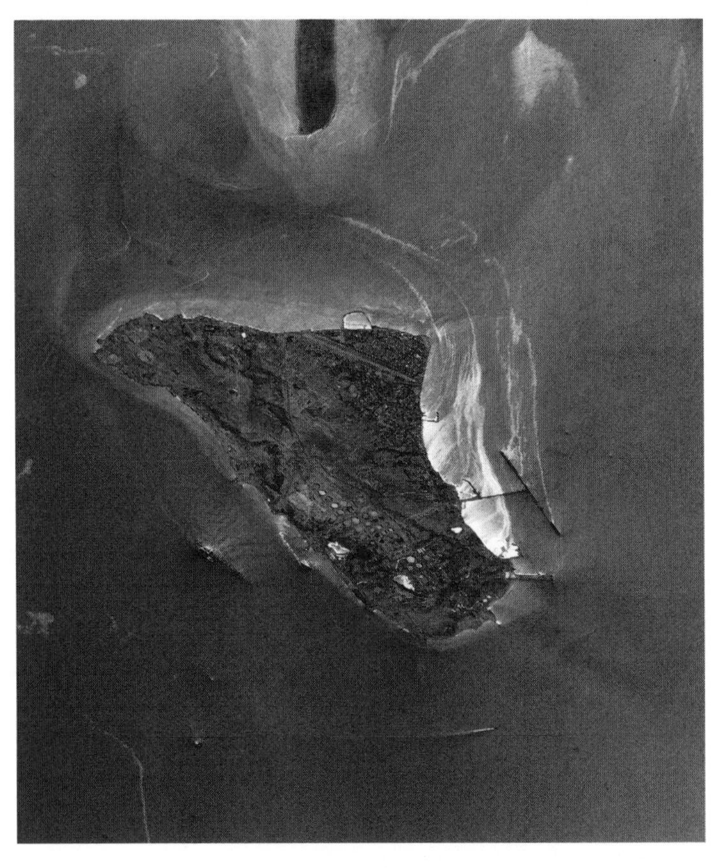

KHARG ISLAND

heated up and it became uncomfortably hot. One never drove across the desert during the hours of darkness, as this was considered far too dangerous. There were no lights on any of the roads, including the major ones, outside the towns and cities. Any local pick-up truck that broke down and this was a frequent occurrence, simply stayed there. The driver would take large rocks and boulders from the side of the road and place them either side of his vehicle, turn off his lights and go to sleep. Anywhere in Europe, markers with reflective tape would be used in place of boulders, so that at least on approach the on-coming driver would have some warning. The number of cars and lorries running into these unlit protecting boulders were countless.

Another danger of driving on desert roads during the hours of darkness was camels. The desert sands rapidly heat up during the day and equally rapidly cool down at night. Camels would come from the desert and find comfort when standing on these roads, as the road surfaces retained heat. Unfortunately, when standing in the middle of the road in pitch blackness, they were a stationary target just waiting to be hit. The main danger to a driver and front passenger, especially those in an ordinary motor car, was that when the camel was struck it's legs would go from under it, and the bulk of a surprisingly heavy body would fall back onto the top of the car, crushing those inside. Many fatalities to both camels and the occupants of vehicles were caused in this way.

Looking back, I think we must have both been a bit mad and a bit irresponsible as parents for doing some of the things we did, and going to some of those places we visited. But we saw a lot of Iran and discovered its captivating beauty. We visited many of the major towns and much of the wilderness of both its mountains and deserts.

On one memorable trip, my wife and I decided to visit the old Silk Road running through Iran from

China to Europe and encompassing the ancient Persian cities of Hamadan and Kermanshah.

The city of Hamadan, situated over 6,000 feet up in the foothills of the Alvand Mountains, has been home to many Persian poets throughout the ages, and was once the capital of the Median Empire. The origins of Hamadan have been dated back to c3000 BC, and it is claimed by many scholars to be one of the oldest continuously inhabited cities of the world. This city is mentioned in the Old Testament book Ezra, and it is thought that Esther, also from the Old Testament, is buried there as well.

We spent one night in Hamadan, and arriving there early afternoon, decided to take a look at some of these truly ancient ruins which lay just outside the city limits. Having spent an enjoyable afternoon meandering around the ruins, we decided we would walk back to our hotel via the Old Town. On approaching the souk, we thought we would take a short cut and entered one of the many shaded side streets.

It was here where we felt the first tingles of tension. Squatting in front of us, spread out all over the pavement were a group of local people whose women had their bodies and faces totally covered. In the heat of the late afternoon, and with the bright sunshine behind us, I was conscious that my tall, slim, fair headed and attractive wife walking beside me was wearing a thin cotton summer dress, which the local women obviously did not approve of. This was definitely a case for prudence and so we crossed to the other side of the street. As we passed, one of the squatting women threw a handful of stones towards my wife; a local insult, to what was perceived as an improperly dressed woman. In all our travels around the Middle East, this was the only time either of us had felt in any way uneasy or uncomfortable.

The following morning we left Hamadan, putting that isolated incident out of our minds, and followed the road over the mountains heading towards Kermanshah. The road we were on was, in fact, part of the Old Silk Route, travelled by that famed explorer of the East, Marco Polo. We thought it would be a good idea, whilst in that area, to see if we could find the internationally renowned and famous bas relief, created on the orders of the Persian King, Darius 1st. We did eventually find it, with a little help from the locals, on the side of a road high up in the mountains. Although it was disappointingly much smaller than we had been led to believe, the inscription on this bas relief (when translated) read his own proclamation: '*Here I am, Darius, King of Kings and Shah of Shahs*'. Thoroughly pleased with ourselves, we continued on through the mountains towards Kermanshah, where we spent the night in one of the many caravansaries - government-sponsored motels - which are scattered throughout the country.

Leaving Kermanshah just after breakfast the following morning, we drove the 400 miles back to Abadan. The road was very steep and narrow in places, winding its way through terrain that was ever changing, from high mountains through gently rolling hills, across an uninteresting plateau, through pastures, until we descended through the Zagros mountain range, to the familiar flat desert leading to the head of the Persian Gulf. There were no detailed road maps of central Iran and we navigated our way around with the help of a school atlas!

Some hours after leaving Kermanshah, in the middle of absolutely nowhere, we came to a fork in the road with another caravansary, a garage and, of course, the mandatory armed National Guardsman idling at his post. Not sure whether we needed to go to the right or left, we stopped and, before I knew it, a loaded rifle was pointed at me through the driver's window. The guard rattled off something in Farsi, the

Iranian language, in which my wife, who was far more a linguist than I could ever be, had been taking lessons. Fortunately, she knew enough of the language to catch the general gist of what he was trying to say. He wanted to ensure that we had sufficient petrol in the car, as the next and nearest garage and petrol station was over 200 miles away! Having resolved that little problem and filled the car's petrol tank to the top, with him watching carefully, we thanked him then invited him to join us for a cup of local tea in the caravansary. The response we received from this young National Guardsman, a simple Iranian lad doing the equivalent of his National Service - for the simple gesture of offering to share a cup of tea with him, was overwhelming - it would have been inconceivable for a young Iranian that a 'ferangi', the foreigner, would pass the time of day with him, let alone not only offer to buy but to share a traditional cup of tea with him.

When we had all finished tea, our new friend returned to his post then, waving him goodbye, we continued our journey southwards, enjoying both the scenery and our remoteness from any habitation...or so we thought. Suddenly the road widened considerably and there was a marked increase in military personnel. We had unknowingly stumbled onto an Iranian Air Force base. The road had been widened to serve as the runway for aircraft landing and taking off. Later, we discovered at that point we were only a few dozen miles from the Iraqi border, and this was at a time when tensions between the two countries were starting to build. It did cross my mind that our newly found friend, with whom we had shared refreshments earlier, might have mentioned this to us. But then of course, it was quite probable he had no idea that an Iranian Air Force base existed there.

On our return to Abadan I went, as usual, down to the oil company's head office to collect any mail that may have arrived whilst we had been away. There the local mail clerk, whom I knew quite well, invited me into his office and immediately asked if everything was well with me, and particularly Mrs Wells? It transpired that whilst we had been travelling in the mountains we had picked up tails from SAVAK - Iran's and the Shah's secret police. One of the tails had witnessed the throwing of stones in Hamadan. A 'quiet' word of warning was given to me to convey to my wife - that perhaps she might dress a little more conservatively in future - as some locals obviously disapproved of young western women wearing semi-transparent dresses. Thereafter, and irrespective of high temperatures and humidity, my wife always made sure that, whenever she went out, she wore a half-slip. Had we been in London, Paris, Rome or New York such an incident would pass without any notice or comment. But we were not in Rome! In many ways this was another interesting lesson in life; when living in a totally different culture to your own, you must always observe all the local customs and guidelines. Had we been in Saudi Arabia, then more likely than not she would have felt the biting sting of the Mutawwa's (religious police) ever present cane that was liberally applied to both locals and foreigners for any such misdemeanour, real or perceived.

For the twenty-one months we lived in Iran we were privileged to see a lot more of the countryside than most expatriates did, simply because my wife and I agreed that life was for living and exploring, both of which we did with great gusto. We found Iran to be not only a place with wonderfully diverse geology, but also a country with a long and distinguished history. We discovered that the Iranians, as a race, were kind and caring people - that one incident in Hamadan aside. In fact, throughout all our travels in the Middle East, we found the vast majority of all the local inhabitants with whom we came in contact to be very friendly, very welcoming and gentle. I think it is correct to say that, in the whole ten years we were there, we only once felt slightly uncomfortable, and perhaps threatened; the same could not be said of either West Africa or the Bahamas!

It was in Iran that I made my first inroads into a sport which has consumed me ever since: golf. Just outside Abadan airport on the road to Khorramshah, there was a desert golf course to which all the expatriate golfers from both towns belonged. It wasn't long before I had been bitten by the golfing bug, and then spent much of my time learning the fundamentals of swinging a club. The concept of both the physics and mechanics of a golf swing I found to be relatively easy. Armed with a second-hand half set of clubs, my initial maximum handicap of 24 became 12 in just a matter of a few months, and I was on my way. With no grass at all on the course, and the greens being constructed from brown oiled sand, I found later in life that 'bunker play' never held any fears!

A VIEW OF ABADAN GOLF COURSE 1973

It was from a chance remark I overheard at the Club that I learned of a vacancy for a marine pilot at the port of Sitra, an oil terminal port further down the Gulf, at Bahrain. A few telephone calls and days later, I flew down to Bahrain via Kuwait for an interview. It was made very clear to the Port Captain that I was a London pilot first and foremost, and that each year I needed to return to London to renew my licence - the rationale behind this was, that Trinity House insisted that every pilot had to perform a minimum number of 'acts of Pilotage' each year in order to maintain the validity of their licence; not dissimilar to the private aeroplane pilots having to fly a minimum number of hours in order to maintain their private pilots licence or PPL as it is known. They were happy with that and so, on returning to Abadan, I resigned and made the necessary arrangements to fly my family down to Bahrain.

When the time came for us to leave Iran we decided to leave from the beautiful and very picturesque city of Shiraz. Leaving Abadan a day early and taking an internal flight to Shiraz, allowed us to spend a full day touring the nearby ancient town of Persepolis. It was on a site just on the outskirts of Persepolis that the Shah of Iran had a purpose-built tented village created, to which he invited every Head of State throughout the world to celebrate 2000 years of Persian/Iranian rule. Many heads of State, including our own Queen Elizabeth 2nd, attended the lavish celebrations which lasted several days.

When the celebrations were finally over, the Shah decreed the tented town should remain in situ. We were amongst the very few British citizens privileged to have had the opportunity to walk around and enter those very same tents, where the world's Royalty and Presidents, and probably a good number of dictators as well, had lived for a few days.

Chapter 7

Bahrain

The Kingdom of Bahrain (Mamlakat al-Barayn) literally translated means the "Kingdom of the Two Seas". It is a relatively small group of coral-based islands situated down in the southern part of the Persian Gulf, and in a bygone age, was the centre for the Persian Gulf's pearl-fishers. A former British stronghold and protectorate, this island Sheikdom was used as a military base.

Situated on the island of Muharraq is Bahrain's International Airport, a stopping off and re-fuelling point for many major airlines passing from Europe to South East Asia and beyond. It was formerly the headquarters of the Royal Air Force Middle East station. Immediately south of Muharraq Island is the main island, simply known as Bahrain, and it is here where the capital Manama is sited with its renowned Bab-el-Bahrain souk.

Bahrain is a constitutional monarchy and the ruler, when we lived there, was Sheik Isa bin Sulman al Khalifa, a genuinely lovely little 'roly-poly' man who was both very pro western and relatively liberal in his outlook. Bahrain came into its own during the late 1970's, when many of the major banks moved from the war torn Middle East financial centre in Beirut to the stability of Bahrain. With its oil reserves low to start with and dwindling rapidly, Bahrain, like the latter day Dubai, decided to expand into other areas and off-shore banking was its first venture.

In many ways Bahrain was still a sleepy little place in the 1970's, it was terribly hot and humid, but nevertheless considered one of the 'better' Persian Gulf Sultanates. Today, instead of being an isolated island nation, Bahrain is joined to its giant neighbour, Saudi Arabia, by a causeway and continues to thrive as one of the more stable, pro-western nations in the whole Persian Gulf area.

Bahrain became the headquarters of the coalition forces when Kuwait was liberated in the early 1990's, and then again a few years later during the 2nd Gulf War.

From Shiraz in Iran, we arrived at Bahrain International Airport, where we were met and whisked away to the oil company town of Awali. Here, much to our total delight, we found the company accommodation allocated to us far exceeded all of our expectations. Awali is situated in the centre of Bahrain's main island and was built by the Bahrain Petroleum Company, BAPCO, for the use of its many expatriate employees.

SITRA'S NORTH TERMINAL

After a week of induction into oil company policies and politics, I was taken to my new Pilotage district, the oil terminals at the Port of Sitra. Already an experienced pilot and ship handler, I had acquired sufficient local knowledge within one month to be granted a licence and then was let loose by myself. In this oil terminal port there was only ever one pilot on duty at any one time, working a shift pattern in conjunction with the oil refinery workers, many of whom, like ourselves, were from the UK.

It took very little time to settle into the rhythm of the port. Our two sons started attending the company's school two minutes walk from our accommodation, and my wife found herself drawn into the social community of expatriate wives. Within a few months she had started teaching at the school, enjoying the same hours and holidays as the boys. It all seemed too good to be true. The first year flew by and, before we knew it, we were on the plane to London, stopping off for a few days in the culturally cosmopolitan city of Istanbul, formerly known as Constantinople and Byzantium.

Istanbul in all its splendour, sitting astride the Bosporus, bridges the continents of Europe and Asia. To our way of thinking it seemed pretty stupid, when the oil company was paying all our airfares back to London, if we didn't take advantage and stop over en-route. This way, when leaving Bahrain on our annual leave, we ended up visiting countries and places we would never ordinarily have had the opportunity to see. Sometimes the planning of our trips was as much fun as the actual trips themselves.

One such episode was when we spent months planning a trip for all four of us to go to New Zealand, where I proudly introduced my English wife and sons to my long lost family. Remarkable as it may seem, it was cheaper for us to fly to London and then on to New Zealand, returning to London and then back to Bahrain. It meant of course we were forced to spend a further 13 hours flying, but the money we saved on airfares gave us more than adequate funds for spending on the trip. The main point of discussion in the initial planning was which way around the world we should go, considering we would have two children with us, both under the age of 8. Before we finally made our bookings, we wrote to the medical department of British Airways, as our main concern was jet lag and how it may affect the boys. The considered opinion was that it would be best if we travelled from Bahrain to London to Los Angeles, then onto Hawaii and finally down to Auckland. Heading back we would go from Auckland to Sydney, Singapore, Doha, London and then back to Bahrain. A very long way, but it worked, and, in all the subsequent trips back home 'down under', we would always travel this way. By heading westward and following the sun, we consequently felt less affected by the time change and jet lag. This was to have a major effect on our thinking and planning a few years later when we were living in the Bahamas. When returning from the Bahamas to boarding school, the boys travelled one day earlier to help them overcome the jet lag commonly experienced when flying between Miami and London.

We had six and a half very happy years living in Awali, Bahrain and the boys grew up in an environment we could never have attempted to replicate had we stayed in England. As a family, we were all very much involved in the social and sporting scene; the desert golf club, where we all took our own little piece of astro turf and, like in Iran, putted on sand 'browns'.

I held several different offices on the committee and got my handicap down to single figures. Then there was the swimming club where my wife ended up as President, in addition to the local amateur dramatics and several sporting activities available for the boys. One of the favourite haunts on a Friday afternoon (the Islamic equivalent of our Sunday) for everybody, both locals and expatriates, was the race course. Great hilarity and enjoyment was experienced by all during the camel races when young Arab boys usually below the age of 12 rode their charges bareback over a roughly hewn desert course. The camels, invariably ignoring the exhortation of their drivers, went off in whatever direction their whim took them.

AWALI GOLF CLUBHOUSE

It was not unknown, during the height of summer, to leave home at 6.30am, go to work with three spare sets of clothing, and return home later that day, wearing the fourth set which was also soaking wet with perspiration. But the houses and cars were geared to those extremes of climate and, of course, life's pace was reduced to a crawl.

Catching a cold in these extremes of heat and humidity was bad news, and many a newly arrived expatriate from the cooler climes of Northern Europe ended up in hospital...with the flu! In the summer time, in order to try and avoid a common cold, we pilots when at work would avoid going into and out from the air-conditioned accommodation. By staying out in the hot humid air, we avoided the continual change of temperature, and thus remained relatively free of the chills that invariably accompanied these drastic variations. During the long, terribly hot and humid summer months, everyone's life was governed by the daytime temperatures, and so many activities - especially the sporting ones - took place in what can only be described as 'unsocial' hours. We would think nothing of rising before dawn and standing on the first tee at the golf club, waiting for and watching the sun rise, knowing we would only manage 9 holes of play before it became too hot. Or we would go to the squash courts at midnight when it was cool enough to play. We not only juggled our sporting activities, but life in general was worked around the extreme climatic conditions in which we lived.

AWALI GOLF CLUB

It was during one long hot and humid summer that Concorde came to Bahrain. Bahrain was chosen for the aircraft to undergo trials with the testing of both landing and taking off in extreme temperatures. The average daily temperatures during August were frequently in the region of 110° F to 120° F, with a corresponding humidity well over 90%. Had I not been recovering from a dislocated shoulder, then we too would have been among those British expatriate residents of Bahrain who were invited to fly Concorde as 'guinea pigs' for training of the cabin crews. But, alas, it was not to be.

January 1976 was when hundreds of British expatriates crowded the observation platform at Bahrain's International Airport to witness the arrival and departure of Concorde's inaugural commercial flight between London and Bahrain. Other great celebrations were always held when, usually towards the end of September, the nightly 'low' temperature fell for the third consecutive night to below 100° F!

Out of the blue and much to my surprise, I received a telephone call one day from the head of the Marine Operations Department, asking if I would be interested in a one year secondment from operations into the training department. I was offered the mandate to set up a training scheme for local tug captains and pilots, both of whom the Bahraini Government wanted, eventually, to take over from the expatriates.

To be quite honest this didn't really appeal to me. The thought of working regular hours and having every weekend off was a bit of a drudge. I had always looked upon those whose work required them to be present at the same place 9 to 5 daily, as having a rather dull existence. But my wife's persuasive powers, playing on both the family aspect and the 'normalisation' of working hours, won the day. Albeit reluctantly, I agreed, and within a couple of weeks found myself sitting in an office with a blank sheet of paper, wondering how I would set up a training schedule from scratch and where to start.

It took some time to adjust and to get used to working regular hours five days a week - not 9 to 5, but 6am to 3pm - however this was an interesting period during which I actually wrote a training manual that the oil company accepted and published in my name. My heart was never fully in it, nor was I really committed to the cause, but having agreed to do it, I persevered to the best of my ability. I was very glad when that year finished and I was able to return to my love of being at the sharp end of piloting and ship handling, even if this required working totally unsocial hours.

BAPCO was a wholly owned subsidiary of the oil giants Caltex and Texaco. Consequently, as both companies ran their own fleet of ships, many of their ships called at the Sitra terminal on a regular basis. We oil terminal pilots got to know the regular captains well and often, whilst their ship was berthed at the oil terminal, there were exchanges and social pleasantries. Wives and families from Awali were invited aboard for dinner, and the ships' captains and their wives were invited ashore for beach parties and BBQ's.

Part of any commercial marine pilot's remit is to advise the captain of any significant local legal requirements and/or customs of the port. In Bahrain, as indeed many other ports throughout the world, having safely berthed or docked the ship, both captain and pilot retired for a quiet beer or two whilst the gangway was being organised and put into position. Frequently during these informal sessions, many bureaucratic cogs and wheels were oiled, and it was all put down on OCS (referred to in chapter 4).

A good number of these ships were regularly trading between Bahrain and Australia as well as

Bahrain and Malaysia and, whilst the ship was at the Sitra terminal loading its cargo of refined oils for these far-flung ports, so the pilots would place their 'food' orders. On the ship's return to Bahrain, it was a common sight to see pilots' cars lined up alongside the jetty whilst crates of various food items were transferred. This way we had a continual supply of spices from Malaysia and, best of all, lobster tails from the Great Barrier Reef. Another supply of fresh meat was the 'sheep ship'. These were mainly older ships converted from their former requirements into mass movers of sheep.

With Britain's entry into the Common Market, many of the established and traditional trades from Australia and New Zealand ceased to exist - virtually overnight. Not only did this have a drastic effect upon the shipping industry, but forced both countries to look for alternate markets. Subsequently there developed a huge trade in both live cattle and sheep to various Middle Eastern countries. Because of the strict Halal guidelines, required by the Islamic faith in the killing of livestock, all the animals were transported live. These ships, accommodating upwards of 20,000 head of sheep or 10,000 head of cattle, frequently called into the Port of Sitra for refuelling.

During the passage from the antipodes to the Middle East there would be numerous births and deaths of the 'passengers', so several cattlemen were employed aboard to help care for the animals. Provided that the berthing of the ship was 'uneventful', and I hasten to say the vast majority were, and before the pilot joined the captain for a drink, one of the cattlemen would be detailed to guide the pilot down to the very smelly cattle decks where a lamb would be selected. This done, the pilot was accompanied back to the ship's bridge where the captain had organised refreshments. Whilst the two were then 'oiling bureaucratic cogs and wheels', the lamb would be slaughtered, dressed and presented to the pilot as he left the ship. A quick telephone call home ensured space in the deep freeze was available, and so we had lamb on the menu for the next few months. It was also surprising at these times how many new friends the pilots of Sitra found they had!

Basking sharks were frequently to be found around the jetties at Sitra, and the tug crews, when they had time on their hands, would go fishing. The Wells household became well known in Awali for 'shark and chip' parties, eaten out of newspapers as well.

Of course all good things in life have a down side, and a difficult time for us was when our eldest son was about to reach the age of 11. We had to decide whether one, or both of us, should return to the UK as the alternative was to send him to boarding school. The situation on the London River was continuing to deteriorate and the immediate prospects of an early return looked bleak, so we decided that we would stay abroad and he would attend school in England.

Several schools were looked at until we finally decided upon Pangbourne College, just outside Reading and not too far from Heathrow. The time came when his mother had to take him to England and place him in the care of his new Housemaster at the Prep school. Having done this, she turned and headed straight back to the airport to catch the next night flight back to Bahrain. What trauma, for both of them! Many other expatriate parents had to undergo this same experience as well, and much advice was available, but experience showed this was by far the best way. The Housemasters at the boarding schools accepting children from expatriate families were well versed in coping with such situations. In a surprisingly short space of time, he soon settled down and started enjoying his newfound freedom.

BAPCO, to whom I was contracted, were excellent employers in many different ways. They not only paid school fees in full but also gave two additional return air tickets each year, so all of the children attending boarding schools in the UK could travel back to Bahrain during the school holidays. We continued to live well and the lifestyle suited us both, as we always took the opportunity to travel extensively. However, all things do come to an end, and after six and a half years it was time to move on. We packed up our belongings once again and this time returned to our home in England.

I spent some time back on the River Thames, but was never fully accepted back into the pilot's roster since there was still simply not enough work to go round. Having no other choice, I looked around for another 'rent a pilot' posting overseas.

Freeport, Bahamas looked promising, but I had to wait nearly five months before all the necessary paperwork was complete. In the meantime there was still a mortgage that had to be paid each month, and so it was off to Jeddah on the Red Sea coast of Saudi Arabia for a three-month single basis contract as Harbour Pilot. It was the first time in nearly eight years that I was alone and away from my family, and I found it surprisingly difficult.

Chapter 8

Jeddah, Saudi Arabia

Saudi Arabia is mostly known as a desert kingdom, sitting on top of the world's greatest oil fields. The Kingdom is sometimes called "The Land of the Two Holy Mosques", referring to both Mecca and Medina, the two holiest places in Islam. The current Kingdom was founded by Adbul-Aziz bin Saud, whose efforts began in 1902 when he captured the Al-Saud's ancestral home of Riyadh, and culminated in 1932 with the proclamation and international recognition of the Kingdom of Saudi Arabia. This is a country where the strictest interpretation of Sharia law is observed.

I can truthfully say that Jeddah was a great port to operate in as a pilot and I thoroughly enjoyed the variation of the work. We were never idle, as the port had over 65 different berths and was always full, with ships arriving and leaving round the clock seven days a week. So busy was the port that there were often, at any one time, up to two dozen ships anchored outside the harbour awaiting a free berth. Big ships, small ships, old ships, new ships; you name them - they were all there. But what did I think of the city of Jeddah? Well, that was something else.

The expatriate pilots, who numbered over 50, were all contracted to the Saudi Arabian Sea Ports Authority (SEAPA) through a major British Middle Eastern Company, Gray MacKenzie, a subsidiary of the Inchape Group. We all lived in an enclosed camp and our living accommodation consisted of groups of self contained portacabins all clustered together. Meals were taken in a large communal mess hall adjacent to the recreational centre. It was a delight to meet up with many of my colleagues from the Port of London who were there for the same reason as I was. Our camp was one of the largest expatriate camps in Jeddah. For not only did Gray MacKenzie employ pilots, but every other type of port worker with the exception of actual dock labour. We all lived in a regimented system and most people, like me, were only there on short-term contracts.

Apart from inside the grounds of the British Embassy, there were no golf courses in Jeddah, and so I had no golf to play. Contract pilots - no matter their golf handicap - were not invited into the Embassy. In my spare time I preferred to drive out from Jeddah into the desert, or lounge either at the pool or on the beaches of the Red Sea coastline. For the first time in my life I spent some time messing around in small sailing boats, but quickly decided that this was not my scene. Always contending that I work on, not in, and definitely not under the sea, the international appeal of scuba diving in the Red Sea reefs off Jeddah held no attraction for me either.

Although I was not personally interested in the popular pastime of distilling 'saddiqi', literally translated into 'my friend', many of the camp residents became quite proficient brewers, who claimed a good concoction was difficult to differentiate from a bottle of Gordon's gin. With plentiful supplies of this illicit alcohol, raucous parties were not unknown and the authorities were content to turn a blind eye, provided that they were all held within the confines of the camp.

About 200 miles up the coast, at a place called Yanbu, a new port and city were being constructed from scratch. This was a town-planners dream - a blank piece of paper, miles of wide open desert and an almost unlimited budget. Gray MacKenzie was going to make a bid for the marine contract, and so I and another pilot, a colleague from London, were sent up there to take a look at the proposed port and write a report. I couldn't have known then that, in a few years time, I would be appointed Deputy Harbour Master at that port. The turnover of expatriate pilots in Jeddah was high, and so I was not at all surprised when, as my contract neared its end, I was offered a long term married status employment contract as a Port Pilot in Jeddah.

This long-term contract came with an excellent salary package; thank you but no thank you! I loved the work but I hated the place, and was very glad when the time came for me to fly back to my family in England. For the first time I could remember, I could not wait to leave and get away from my place of work. My wife and youngest son were at Heathrow to meet me after we landed, and I remember thinking how glad I was to be back in Old Blighty, 'orrible weather and all. A couple of weeks were spent operating on the River Thames to maintain the validity of my pilot licence, but there was little enough movement in the Port to warrant full time return. Even with no likelihood of any immediate work on the Thames, I had at least my Trinity House River Thames pilot's Licence renewed for a further year.

I cannot describe the euphoria both my wife and I felt when finally the letter arrived, informing us that our papers were all in order and we should prepare to fly out to the Bahamas. Fortunately, there was sufficient time before flying to the Bahamas for me to make a quick trip back to New Zealand and visit my ailing mother. A non-stop flight from London to Auckland via Los Angeles and Honolulu is never fun, but time constraints did not allow any leeway for stopovers and so it had to be done. The flight was remarkably uneventful and I managed to spend two weeks with my mother as we toured around the North Island of New Zealand as any tourist would. Saying goodbye to her at Auckland's International Airport, I set off for the long flight to Freeport, Bahamas, stopping over at San Francisco where I changed to a USA internal flight bound for Miami, and then onwards to Freeport.

Chapter 9
The Bahamas

How evocative are these words: "The Bahamas" - heaven on earth? Having lived there for almost four years, I think not!

The Commonwealth of the Bahamas consists of approximately 2000 small uninhabited cays (pronounced keys) and 700 islands, many of which are also not inhabited, and they stretch several hundreds of miles southeast of Florida.

Since attaining independence from the UK in 1973, the Bahamas have prospered through tourism, international banking and investment management. But because of its geography and isolated and uninhabited islands, the country was a major trans-shipment point for illegal drugs, and its territory was used for smuggling illegal migrants into the US. It was and still remains a 'safe' tax haven for the rich and famous.

Having arrived at Miami exhausted and suffering from jet lag, I met up with my wife and our younger son who had flown out from London the day before. After a good night in bed, the following day we caught one of the dozen or so daily flights across to Freeport - a short flight of only about 40 minutes. As we swept in over the coral reefs and lagoons of Grand Bahama Island (GBI) we thought how wonderful it all looked yet, once again, little did we know what lay in store for us during the following four years. Looking back on those years we lived abroad, the most difficult of all our postings, including Saudi Arabia, was in fact Freeport, GBI, Bahamas.

I started work the following day, this time for my new employers NEPCO (New England Petroleum Company), who had the contract for all marine operations at the Bahamas Oil Refinery Company (BORCO). My wife started teaching at the local International school the following week, where our younger son would attend. It was then that I appreciated why it made sense for some overseas companies to insist on expatriate pilots going to their new posting ahead of their family, because until licensed and cleared to operate within the port and sea terminals, life was pretty chaotic.

After only a few short but hectic weeks to absorb the relatively easy geography of the Port of Freeport, before I knew it I was back 'on watch' working a constant pattern of 12 hours on duty, then 12 hours off, another 12 hours on duty followed by 24 hours off. Repeating that rota was followed by four whole days off. Lots of spare time was to be had for me. Meanwhile my wife was struggling to come to grips with a curriculum containing the best of both British and US education systems.

Many of the ships we handled and docked were technically interesting, in that they were fully laden - and consequently extremely heavy 'very large crude carriers' (VLCC's), that is to say roughly between 200,000 and 300,000 tons - or the 'ultra large crude carriers' (ULCC's), which are 300,000 tons and upwards. We also handled many of the prestige passenger liners, some of which were in the process of being converted into cruise ships. So, on those occasions when I returned to the Port of London to retain my River Thames licence, the ships we handled there seemed so small after the giants I was now used to handling out in the Bahamas.

Having so much spare time on my hands, it was easy to spend much, perhaps too much, time out on one of the many top class golf courses which were scattered across the island. Now that I was playing golf on proper grass courses, within no time my handicap was well down into low single figures. I soon found myself co-opted onto the committee of the club where I had become a member: Bahamas Princess Golf and Country Club – a club boasting more millionaires than Woburn, Wentworth and Sunningdale combined. Within a year, I was Club Captain and then for the remaining two years, Club President. When playing off a handicap of 3 (2.8) I was invited to join the South Florida Amateur Circuit. As the working patterns of the Port's pilots allowed ample time for ourselves, it was relatively easy to fly across to Florida to play in this high standard top amateur golf circuit. For those who understand golf, the format played was 'scratch stableford' with a maximum entry handicap of 4...a hard school!

Following on from the Princess Golf Club and the Amateur Circuit in Florida, it was not long before I was invited to join the Board of the Bahamas Professional Golf Association (BPGA). I understand that I remain the only white non-Bahamian to have ever been offered this privilege. Consequently, I found that even more time was spent both playing as well as weaving in and out of the golfing politics, and so the foray into the port to go to work was often a welcome interlude!

By the end of our second year in Freeport, our younger son had joined his brother at boarding school back in Pangbourne, Berkshire. Naturally we missed the bustle of having the boys around, but this was a great life. My wife, however, whose work bound her to the Island, found life far more difficult and demanding.

It was on the flight back to London on our first leave from Freeport that my wife stated, quite firmly, that if there was still no sign of business picking up on the Thames, I should investigate the possibility of getting another posting back in the Middle East. She would prefer to be there living in the Middle East rather than in Freeport, Bahamas! What? After all the fabulous golf courses in both Florida and the Bahamian islands, go back to those 'desert' golf courses? Not likely!

BALANCED FINISH!

The flight back to London from Miami takes, on average, seven hours and, with a time difference of five hours, so most people arrive at Heathrow feeling, jaded, tired and jet lagged. In an earlier chapter, I referred to the time when we spent ages deciding which way around the world we should fly on our first trip to New Zealand from Bahrain. The time we spent, the research carried out plus our own first hand experiences all now paid dividends - when the boys were returning to school in England, flying eastwards against the clock, we always sent them at least one day early so that they could stay with relatives, as this meant that they had an extra day or two before returning to the classroom.

The difference in visiting the Bahamas as a tourist and living there as an expatriate, were worlds apart. Life in the Bahamas, generally speaking for white expatriates, was definitely not an easy one. Local crime was a major problem as was the drug scene, racial tensions, religious difficulties and so on. There were places on the island where, big and ugly as I may have been, it would not have been safe for me to venture.

A professional colleague, who had left the Manchester Ship Canal to become an expatriate pilot, was found floating face down in one of the many man-made canals that were cut through GBI. Whilst he was still tripping for his local licence, he had badly sprained his ankle when disembarking a ship in heavy weather. After a period of rest he was advised to exercise his ankle as much as possible, and went off walking along a beach that most of us would avoid. Although never completely proven, it was concluded that he was on this beach at the wrong time and probably witnessed a haul of drugs, or something similar, being brought ashore. The men in that business were dangerous and desperate and they never left anything to chance. He had to be silenced... literally. Our Port Manager must have had a difficult time when he telephoned the dead pilot's wife and broke the sad news to her. She and their teenage daughter were scheduled to fly out from the UK the following week to start their new life in the Bahamas.

Saturday nights were a particularly dangerous time for many of the package holiday makers, affectionately known as the 'snow birds', who would be returning to their homes in northern United States or Canada the following day. A last flutter before leaving the Island may well have been spent in the casino and a few dollars won. Word would be passed from the inside and, on leaving the casino building, it was not unknown for tourists to be held up at gunpoint, the man beaten and robbed and, if his wife objected, she was raped, if not beaten as well. As the majority of package holidaymakers left the Island on a Sunday in order to return to their place of work on the Monday, there were very few people who would remain on the Island to try and find, and then identify their attackers, let alone press charges.

I distinctly remember one night when making my way home after a golf club committee meeting, I was walking alone down the covered walkway towards the casino when I passed a well dressed local man walking in the opposite direction. As we passed he turned and asked me: "*You want coke man?*" Here I was, this former ship's captain and experienced world traveller, a man of the world and with no idea of what was on offer! It was not until I returned home and told my wife, that it dawned on me the man was a dealer and was offering me drugs. Laugh if you like, but my actual answer, I am somewhat amused today to admit, was: "*No, it's ok thanks, I'm not thirsty*". This was a side of the Bahamas that the Bahamian Tourist Board, of course, always vigorously denied ever existed.

Having lived a somewhat nomadic style of life for so many years and in so many different countries, I remain convinced that although there will always be a down side and some bad times, there is always some good to be found no matter where one may be. And it was like that for us in the Bahamas. We both still retain some wonderful memories of the time we spent living there. Today the Bahamas has managed to erase much of the darker sides to its character and remains a great, if somewhat expensive, place to visit.

Eventually, I was made up to one of the port's senior pilots responsible, on a watch (shift) pattern, for the entire port and the on-watch personnel. Surprising as it may sound, one of the biggest headaches that the senior watch pilots encountered was the weather. The large oil tanker berths were in open water outside the actual harbour of Freeport, where the seas could build up very quickly. In the event of weather fronts, storms and even hurricanes passing through our area, the oil berths had to be evacuated of both ships and personnel. Working in conjunction with the weather centre in Miami, the weather was very closely monitored. Generally speaking, what weather Miami experienced, Freeport would get three or four hours later. Any decision relating to the weather a senior Pilot had to make was always pressurised. We were damned if we did nothing and the subsequent movement of the ship alongside the jetty caused damage, and we were damned if we closed and vacated the terminals and the expected bad weather did not materialise, because that cost the oil company countless thousands of dollars in lost revenue. These were balancing acts which most of the time we got right, but it certainly was not unknown for it to go spectacularly wrong.

There was one night when the local weather was experiencing some strange patterns, caused by the El Nino (warming) effect of the Pacific Ocean. Weather fronts formed without warning and several, which we had been warned of, never materialised. The duty senior pilot was becoming increasingly frustrated as he tried to judge and foretell what weather was expected at our terminal within the next few hours. However, the refinery duty manager - having other problems on his mind, like running out of oil storage space - was insistent the ships be kept alongside the jetties and continue loading their oil cargoes for as long as possible.

This was typical of the commercial pressures exerted on each of the senior pilots, especially during the winter months. As so often happens in these critical situations, the senior pilot on duty that night was relatively new into the job and was, we other senior pilots thought, more concerned about not offending or causing a scene, so he would often go out of his way to appease or accommodate the wishes of others - not a good combination for a senior decision maker! Needless to say, in the wee small hours of that night, the forecasted gale started to blow causing the sea to rise steeply and swiftly, allowing no opportunity to vacate the berths. Even super tankers 'range', that is to say move up and down as well as along the jetties in bad weather, as was proven by two of the tankers that night. After a couple of hours the weather abated as quickly as it blew up and, as soon as the sea subsided, a damage inspection was necessary. Oh dear, it's surprising what damage a half loaded super tanker can do to a jetty. Both of those berths were out of service for several months whilst permanent repairs were carried out. Our poor colleague, not long after that incident, thought perhaps he should look for pastures new!

The large oil tankers moored alongside the offshore jetties had their oil cargoes pumped either ashore to the refinery for processing or, either directly or indirectly, to another ship. The cargoes being transferred indirectly to another ship would be pumped ashore through a loop system passing through the refinery and returned to the ship at the offshore jetty. This provided great advantages not only for the giant oil companies but for governmental agencies as well.

Any cargo coming from the shore had its Bill of Lading marked 'exported from Freeport, GBI, Bahamas', which was one of the ways the American government got around its own embargo of preventing anything entering into the United States from Libya (and other embargoed countries). Ships would arrive in

Freeport from Libyan ports filled to the brim with crude oil. The oil would be pumped ashore around the refinery and directly back offshore to a waiting tanker who would load that cargo and then sail off to the United States with a cargo of crude oil from Freeport, Bahamas. Was this ingenious or just another underhand capitalistic method of bucking the system?

Although primarily an oil tanker port, Freeport also had its fair share of other ships calling there. The *QE2* was a regular visitor, as was *the Canberra* and *the Norway* (formerly *the France*), which at that time was the world's largest passenger ship. I was privileged to handle all three on many of their visits. A well-known Danish shipping company, DFDS, had set up a daily ferry service between Freeport and Miami. They employed an old Ro-Ro (Roll on–Roll off) ferry that was designed and built to trade between Scandinavian ports. Because she was heavily insulated to keep the cold out, and lacked many windows that opened out onto the open decks, she was quite unsuitable for working in the warmer climes of the Bahamas and Florida.

One of the nice regular perks we pilots had was, having sailed this ferry from Freeport Harbour, we stayed aboard for the trip across to Miami. The following day we would return, and as the ship approached the entrance to Freeport we would put our uniform back on, proceed to the ship's bridge, then pilot her back into the Harbour. This service was also offered by the Miami pilots on the reciprocal passage. It was not in the ferry company's interest to lose time by slowing down to embark and disembark pilots, particularly during the winter months when the weather and seas were so unpredictable, so they offered and we gratefully received not only their wonderful Scandinavian hospitality, but an additional inducement to go away for 18 hours. Each of the Freeport pilots took it in turn to perform this task on our days off duty.

The largest commercial merchant ship ever built to sail the oceans of the world, a ship which was severely damaged by Iranian exocet missiles during the Irani/Iraqi war with heavy loss of life, was also a regular visitor to our port. If you remember, we've already mentioned this ship in an earlier chapter and when fully laden with oil, fuel and stores, the *Jahre Viking*, if it were possible to lift her out of the water, would weigh in at a mere 825,000 tons. And just think, she travelled around the world at about 15 mph and without brakes! When she and other similarly large and heavy oil tankers were being berthed, on the final run-in approach to the jetty, transit markers on the shore showed us when we had just 1½ miles to go to where the ship needed to be stopped. If the ship was doing 2 knots, that is marginally over 2 mph, then things were a bit on the fast side and the speed had to be reduced, or the ship was in danger of overrunning the berth. When handling these large and heavy ships, not only is the speed that critical, but then so is the skill, knowledge, experience and the temperament of the pilot!

The American nuclear aircraft carrier *USS Nimitz* is one in a class of warships which are the biggest ever built. When she arrived at Freeport, she had in excess of 6,600 officers and crew with numerous combat aircraft and helicopters aboard. Her flight deck measures over four acres in area. Today this ship is still in commission and it is estimated that her nuclear fuel allows her to remain at sea whilst steaming at full speed for a period of 24 years - yes, that's right, twenty-four years, without having to refuel. I once piloted this giant nuclear powered aircraft carrier into and out of Freeport. When I got on board and finally reached the navigation bridge, I looked out across the sprawling deck covered with countless aircraft, and the sheer size took my breath away. I had been used to large heavy ships but nothing on this scale before.

On meeting the captain on the bridge, we adjourned to the chartroom situated at the back of the wheelhouse where a berthing conference took place. Had this been a small coastal ship, the amount of gold braid present at that conference may well have endangered the stability of the ship! The first question the captain asked, and quite rightly so, was what my experience was when it came to handling these huge ships. I was almost tempted to say something like, "*well Captain, this is my first day on the job*", but somehow I didn't think that would go down very well, even if said in jest! Holding the centre stage I, with much more confidence than I felt, spelled out the manoeuvre I was about to undertake. Back out in the wheelhouse the captain in his slow Texan drawl stated to no one in particular but to everybody present that "*the pilot has the con*", meaning it was now all mine. In all the years I have been in command and the thousands of ships I have been aboard as the operating pilot, I have never felt quite as insecure as I did at that moment.

As the captain heaved himself up and into his command chair, he touched me on the sleeve and said these words, which I remember distinctly to this day: "*hey Cap, whatever you do please don't bend my ship*". Where do I go from here I thought but, using all the tugs available in the port, the ship was docked without even a scratch on her paintwork. A few days later I even managed to get her out of port again without a mark...but a lot more grey hairs!

There is an old saying at sea and especially in Pilotage services: "*The smaller the ship, the bigger the captain*" and this generally refers to the size of the captain's head!"

The captain of the Nimitz was about to be promoted to the Flag Rank of Rear Admiral and had nothing to prove, for he had already shown several times that he had managed to have his massive ship enter and leave different ports without incident or damage. So he was quite happy, having established my record of service as a pilot, to sit back, watch, and let me get on with it. There are many senior ship Masters and Commanding Officers of warships who share the same quiet confidence in both themselves and their pilot, but on the other hand, oh, it can be so different!

For example, a few years later I was back in London full time: One Saturday afternoon I was detailed to join a small 1,500 ton continental coaster inbound for Dagenham, about 11 miles up river from Gravesend. It was a fine day with little wind, good visibility and only a moderate tide running. As I arrived up on the bridge, I gave my usual cheery "*Hello*

Captain and welcome to London, I hope you've had a good voyage", only to be met by a sullen, scruffy looking individual with an obvious chip on his shoulder, who replied, "*I have been coming to London for years and in spite of your new rules, I don't need a pilot*". A great way to start an hour and a half passage up the river! So biting my tongue, I smiled and gave my stock answer to such characters. "*That's fine by me captain, you go ahead...you obviously need the experience a lot more than I do*". A sure conversation stopper, but although infrequent, I had met these types before.

The weather and tidal conditions were good and there was not too much traffic around on the river at that time, so, provided he kept his ship in the middle of the river, there was little harm he could come to. As we progressed up the river I made the appropriate radio calls to London Port Control indicating our progress. After about 30 minutes into the passage Frau Kapitan, who was sitting in the corner of the wheelhouse quietly knitting, and who had obviously seen this situation all too often at other ports, came across to me smiling and asked if I would like a cup of coffee, which I gratefully accepted.

TYPICAL CONTINENTAL COASTER

In any such difficult circumstances I always thought it prudent, when speaking to London Port Control, to inform the Duty Officer about the situation on board and would ask him to monitor their radars, but not to call us or say anything over the open airwaves.

With his Carl Zeiss binoculars strung around his neck, the Captain gave every impression of being a second world war U-Boat commander. However, his body language was starting to show signs of some uncertainty. When the captain committed, what any self-respecting licensed pilot considers a totally unforgivable sin, I knew the advantage had swung to me. Emerging from the chartroom at the back of the bridge, our captain brought with him his chart of the River Thames. After several apparently detailed examinations of his chart, then peering through his binoculars, he finally turned to me and said "*It is a long while since I was this far up the river and the skyline seems to have changed a lot*". To which I replied "*Well captain it is true, London's skyline is virtually changing almost daily and that, dare I say, is why the law states each ship must have an experienced pilot aboard who is fully aware of all changes*".

Eventually Teutonic pride was swallowed and he asked me to indicate which one was Dagenham Dock berth number 6. With as much antipodean diplomacy as I could muster, I smiled sweetly and said, "*Number 6 berth? Why yes captain that is the one you passed...nearly two miles back!*" Much to the amusement of the on duty staff watching their radars at the Port Control Centre and myself, this arrogant little man had to suffer the ignominy of turning his ship around before proceeding back down river to his allotted berth. I took no real delight in his embarrassment but it did show that no matter which port in the world you may be visiting, and no matter how often you may have called there, there is simply no substitute for both local knowledge and the experience of the district pilot.

The worst captains were those who were physically too short to see over the windbreakers on the ship's bridge wings and had to have stools made for them to stand on. Give a physically little man command and authority...!

Back in the Bahamas in the mid 1980's, world wide economic uncertainties led to BORCO having to make cut backs and shut down part of their refinery plant. As I was one of the more expensive expatriate pilots with my country of origin now classified as New Zealand rather than England, I was one of the first to go. The difference in country of origin meant the oil company had to pay airfares for four of us from Freeport to New Zealand and not England. So, quite out of the blue, one morning on going to work I was summoned into the Port Manager's office to be told that my services were no longer required, and I was to be terminated forthwith. I was accompanied to my office and personal locker by one of the security guards and then escorted off the premises. Somewhat taken aback, not so much by the termination of my contract, but at the inept and unpleasant way it was handled, I thought to myself, wow, the American way can be brutal.

I had to telephone and break the news to my wife, who had only just flown back to London a couple of days earlier to attend a major event at our sons' school. We talked it over and decided not to do anything too quickly, so she returned to Freeport where we spent three weeks on holiday before once more packing up our home. It was surprising how differently we felt being in the islands as holidaymakers and not as workers, because my wife had to resign her post at the school - her local work permit was issued only on the strength that I was engaged in full time employment and in possession of a valid work permit myself which, of course, was now null and void.

As I was still smarting at the manner in which the termination of my contract had been handled, I decided to call in a few IOU's. My wife and I were on friendly terms with the local Chief of Police and his wife, who was the Headmistress at the International school where my wife taught. As President of the Bahamas Princess Golf and Country Club I had helped facilitate the Chief's honorary membership into the golf club, and we would often play a round of golf together. It was the same Chief of Police who would occasionally organise a discreet telephone call suggesting neither of us should be present in a certain place or around at a certain time. Bearing in mind the fate of our colleague from the Manchester Ship Canal, we took advantage of having friends in high places. He and I had a long chat about my situation, after which we decided it best if I quietly accepted what was on offer, take the money and go. This is what we did, leaving Freeport with a suitcase full of US Dollars and a bad taste in our mouths. In spite of this, some of the many local and expatriate peoples we had met and made friends with still remain friends to this day.

This was a pivotal time in our lives as our eldest son was away on his gap year before returning to read for his degree in transport, and our younger son was finishing his 'O' levels, having great aspirations of going to medical school, which he eventually did. Sadly, my wife and I, who had been living rather separate lives for the previous couple of years, decided to go our separate ways, albeit for a period of time, to see how things worked out.

In some ways we both felt a sense of relief that we were leaving the balmy shores of the islands of the Bahamas. Throughout the period of time we lived there, it seemed every expatriate was living on a knife-edge as well as under a continual cloud of tension. In all my subsequent travels I have only returned to the Bahamas once, and that was whilst aboard a cruise ship on which I was lecturer.

It was in the 1980's and the British government of the day were engaged in a long and bitter dispute with the miners, printers and a few other groups including Trinity House, as they had grand plans for the total re-organisation of the British Pilotage Service. So, with little prospects of regular work on the Thames, it was time to look further afield again, and so it was back to the telephones and calling on old contacts.

A few weeks later I was once again winging my way across the skies, this time back to Saudi Arabia, initially to Jeddah and then a further couple of hundred miles or so north up the coast to the new King Fahd Industrial Port at Yanbu, where I took up an office appointment on a bachelor basis as the Deputy Harbour Master responsible for Pilotage and all local navigational aids. The contractors were the Port of London Authority, who ultimately became my employer, post 1988. London's Port Authority was also experiencing difficult times and had branched out into consultancy work and this was one of their first major contracts. The PLA were responsible to the Saudi Seaports Authority (SEAPA) for overseeing marine contractors in many of their newly emerging ports and harbours.

Chapter 10

Yanbu, Saudi Arabia

On the north west coast of Saudi Arabia is the man-made Yanbu King Fahd Industrial Port and its accompanying city, both a few miles south of the original town and port of Yanbu al Bahr. Jubail, another man-made port and city is situated on the south east coast of Saudi Arabia, and was built to complement Yanbu.

For the following eighteen months my working schedule meant that I was flown out to Saudi for 12 weeks, followed by 4 weeks leave back in the UK. Initially the job was a bit of a novelty, but it didn't take long to become bored by the regular hours and weekends off. So I tried, as often as I could, to get out of the office and work 'hands on' with the pilots. All in all it was interesting enough, as initially I had to set up a training course, and then became chief examiner for all expatriate pilots and much time was spent flying between Yanbu, Jeddah and Riyadh.

Similar to Jeddah, we all lived in a camp made up of a number of portacabins, surrounded by high walls, one of which had a gate leading to the beach. In many ways this was even more of a 'hardship' posting than Jeddah a few years earlier. Although Yanbu Industrial port and its surrounding city were brand new, they lacked any sort of character. This was, supposedly, a town planner's dream - to be given an unlimited pot of money, wide open desert and a blank sheet of paper on which to create a city.

Living at Yanbu was hard. Not only did we have to commute through the desert each day from our base camp to the Industrial port about 12 miles to the south, but any 'entertainment' was in the new city, 15 miles to the south. One day I had to return to the camp during the morning, for reasons I cannot recall, but on driving in I was confronted by hordes of Saudi police. It appeared that, not only had our Indonesian cook run amok and killed one of the Indian stewards with a cleaver, but the camp manager, who was British, had tried to drag the body out of the compound so that it would be found on public land and not in a private expatriates' compound. After quite a few awkward minutes of explaining why I was returning to the camp at that time of day, as well as convincing the police that I really did not have anything to do with either the murder or moving of the body, I beat a hasty retreat back to the safety of the port. Informing my colleagues of the situation back at the camp, we all gave up our lunch break and stayed at the Port for the remainder of the day!

Another incident worth remembering involved my friend and colleague Jim, the Deputy Harbour Master (Administration) with whom I shared an office.

In those days expatriates were loosely classified. For example, as I had spent most of my expatriate years in the Persian Gulf region, I was classified as a 'Middle East' person. Others were 'Far Eastern' or 'African', depending on how much time they had spent in those areas. Jim was classed as 'African', having spent countless years working in various African countries and their ports. One of the fundamental differences between a 'Middle East-man' and an 'African-man' was that in Africa the local laws were, generally speaking, very lax, if ever applied. In the Middle East, and especially Saudi Arabia, the local laws were not only very strict but also rigorously applied, to both the local and foreigner alike. Public indulgence in any form of alcohol consumption was classified as one of the more serious breaches. As in Jeddah, parties where alcohol was consumed were quite frequent, but most sensible people never drove home, choosing instead to spend the night in the accommodation provided by their hosts.

Poor Jim was not used to such constraints, and decided one evening to return back to camp, having spent most of the afternoon with other bachelor expatriates sampling the various brews of saddiqi which were all too readily available. Although not drunk, he was, nevertheless, 'under the influence' and was stopped by the police at a routine road block. The first we heard of his problem was when the British Consul called to say that Jim was in jail pending a court appearance. In due course he was sentenced to six months in prison, followed by twelve lashes and deportation. In the overall picture of Saudi sentences for such crimes, this could be considered to be relatively lenient – if you were not the prisoner, that is. We would visit Jim each Thursday and Friday, the Islamic weekend, taking with us both food and money. Food was not provided to the inmates and the money allowed him the small luxuries of cigarettes, water and paying off would-be attackers. It was hell on earth for him and each weekend when we visited he seemed even more shrunken and depressed. Jim, being the only westerner at the time in that particular jail, shared an open cell 20ft x 15ft with up to 40 other convicted men - arsonists, rapists, and even a murderer, in conditions that we would have deemed unsuitable to have kept a dog in. There were no beds or mattresses, there was one water tap everyone had to share, and a hole in the middle of the cell that acted as an open loo for all inmates.

Jim was considered to have been very lucky, for he ended up being reprieved in the King's annual pardon. Having spent three months locked away, he received only ten lashes, was deported and made 'persona non grata' to the Kingdom of Saudi Arabia. This case was made very public throughout the Kingdom as the authorities were always looking for some way of making their point, and this proved another very salutary and deliberate lesson for all expatriates living in the region.

But it was not all gloom and doom. Again with no golf courses and having nothing better to do with my free time, I joined the local amateur dramatic society, 'The Yanbu Players' as we were grandly called. Apart from making a fool of myself on stage by taking part in a Gilbert and Sullivan production, I also had a lot of fun when the society, very courageously, produced Offenbach's 'Orpheus in the Underworld'. Having successfully completed a week's running performance of 'Orpheus' and with a long weekend holiday looming, it was decided that those members who were adventurous, brave or foolhardy enough, would all go off into the desert and visit Mada'in Saleh. This ruined city is situated in North West Saudi Arabia, and was once part of the Nabatean Kingdom whose capital city was Petra in modern day Jordan. Mada'in Saleh was the southern sister city to Petra, and famous in its own right for more than 80 rock-cut tombs and wind carved soft sandstone. Not many westerners, apart from archaeologists, have ever visited there and unlike Petra, Mada'in Saleh was never colonised by the Romans.

WIND CARVED SANDSTONE TOMB

Having obtained all the necessary travel permits from the Ministry of the Interior, it proved to be an interesting journey out into the desert with a convoy of six four wheel drive cars. All the motorway signs in Saudi Arabia conformed to the international road signage of white lettering on a blue background. The road signs on all major roads and motorways were tri-lingual: Arabic, English and French. When approaching the outskirts of Islam's second most holy city, Medina, we were amused to read the signposts. Translated, the Arabic sign read: *'The Faithful bear right to the Holy City of Medina. All other traffic and Infidels bear left'.* Being infidels, we bore left and continued on the by-pass. Most expatriates in the Kingdom of Saudi Arabia eventually came to believe that traffic lights were in place only to make us, the foreigners, feel at home. The locals never took a blind bit of notice if the lights showed green or red; they blithely drove straight on regardless!

Further up country we drove for many miles alongside the railway track made famous when Lawrence of Arabia and his men kept blowing it up during the Arab Revolt of 1916 - 1918. This railway line ran across the harsh deserts between Damascus and Medina, a length of 820 miles.

DERELICT RAILWAY REPAIR SHEDS

REMAINS OF RUSTING ENGINE

The three nights we were away we camped in tents out in the open desert, which brought back memories of my boy scout days in New Zealand, so many years and miles away. The difference between camping out in Saudi and New Zealand was that, amongst the many other things we had to remember, every time we climbed into our sleeping bags we always had to check whether scorpions or other equally unfriendly creatures had gone to bed there first.

Throughout our adventurous journey, where the sight of a westerner was very much a novelty, we were met with unfailing courtesy, politeness, generosity and to a degree, curiosity. At all the military roadblocks we encountered, which were also manned by members of the Mutawwa - Saudi's religious police - as well as every local person we encountered during that long weekend as we drove through the wilderness of Saudi Arabia, there was not one moment when any of our team, the women included, felt threatened or uncomfortable. While there will always be a few hot-headed zealots who spoil and degrade the image of both the people and their nations, most of the ordinary men and women in the majority of the dozens of countries I have visited in my life have been considerate and kind. It never ceases to amaze me how adaptable the human spirit is.

For the eighteen months I was working in Yanbu, we lived as though we were back at sea, with regular, almost at times monotonous routines, but instead of being confined on board ship, we had the freedom of living ashore.

CAMPING IN SAUDI DESERT

I was not sorry when this contract was completed, for I needed a spell back in England to resolve some growing personal problems, as well as keeping my ear to the ground about the major changes that were about to be unleashed on the Pilotage Service throughout the UK.

Chapter 11

Deep Sea Pilotage

On my final flight away from Saudi Arabia, I flew down to the United Arab Emirates, visiting the countries of Abu Dhabi, Dubai and Sharjah. I then drove across the desert hills and sand dunes to Oman to see what work might be available. There was nothing on offer.

I was back at Trinity House renewing my London Pilot's Licence when I was informed, with the impending changes looming over the horizon for the Pilotage service, that the House was not only going to maintain control over licensing of Deep Sea Pilots, but that there was currently a shortage of them.

Each port, by the law of the land, adjusted by local port by-laws, require all ships of a certain size, when entering and leaving port as well as when moving around in the port from one berth or dock to another, to have a local licensed pilot on board. It is not surprising that the underwriters at Lloyds of London are very much in favour of this as well. These compulsory port pilots are known as District pilots, operating only within the geographical limits of that port.

There is another group of pilots known as Deep Sea Pilots (DSP), who are licensed by Trinity House, and operate the long haul routes through the English Channel, Dover Straits and North Sea. Although not required by law to have a DSP on board, many shipping companies, mainly with third world officers and crews, do. Those ships which are not regular visitors to northern European waters, frequently liked to have a Deep Sea licensed pilot on board as well. With their extensive knowledge of the entire area, they assist the ship's captain through some of the busiest shipping lanes and amongst the most treacherous waters in the world.

Other regular users of DSPs are the large container ships calling at seven or eight ports in as many days. Because it is physically impossible for the ship's captain to be on the bridge throughout the passage between ports, and then be available for dealing with all the port officials, accompanying paper work, plus the one hundred and one things required from a ship's captain when he is in port, many employ the services of DSPs.

It works like this: The deep sea pilot comes aboard at Brixham or Cherbourg, for example, and guides the ship to her first port of call where he is then relieved by the local district pilot who takes the ship into port.

PILOT CUTTER

When the ship sails and the local district pilot disembarks, the DSP takes command of the ship guiding her again to the next port where the local district pilot embarks. It is during that period of time when the ship is on passage between ports, that the captain can get his rest. He returns to his bridge as the local pilot is embarked and for entry into port, where he is available to meet all the officials who board. Throughout the ship's stay in port, it is the turn of the DSP to rest. The roles reverse again when the ship sails.

GOING TO WORK

The District pilot will generally embark the ship in a manner most appropriate to his status and importance - a free flowing rope ladder is thrown over the ship's side, which he must climb up and down. The DSP by contrast, often joins and leaves his ship whilst she is still in port, and has a casual climb up the ship's gangway. In some cases though, the DSP is flown by helicopter from ports like Cherbourg to the ship, and vice versa, whilst the ship continues to steam at full speed and is well out in the English Channel. On a cold wet windy night, this could be a frightening operation and is always guaranteed to get the nerves a-jingling!

The work of a DSP is not necessarily as concentrated as his counterpart, the local District pilot, but does involve very long hours on duty on the bridge throughout the sea passage, often in excess of twenty-four hours without a break. Candidates for any District pilot's licence within the UK is usually a Master Mariner but not necessarily have experienced actual command. The candidate for a DSP Certificate must be able to show that he has experienced a minimum of two years in command of an ocean going ship. I already had all the necessary qualifications to sit for a DSP licence.

In order to familiarise myself with these waters before applying for a DSP licence, I was fortunate enough to be offered a temporary four month command of a 4,500 ton cargo ship *m.v. Teme*, engaged in a regular trade between East Germany, Denmark and Morocco. This was a small one-ship company registered in Gibraltar. Consequently the standards, to which I was accustomed and expected, were not necessarily the standards I found on board! This ship was - putting it nicely - basic, offering only the bare minimum required by Gibraltarian law, but somehow we managed. For example, the main navigational equipment we had on board consisted of a simple magnetic compass, one out of date, although functional, radar and a wireless directional finder; a relic from the 1950's. Not for us were there any sophisticated accurate satellite computer navigation and automatic steering systems! This was quite an arduous trade for a relatively small ship, especially during the winter months. We would load our general cargoes in East Germany and Denmark and sail through the icy waters of the Baltic Sea, down through the North Sea, across the ever dangerous Bay of Biscay and then down the unprotected Iberian coastline, frequently ending up fighting the huge swells that are regularly found off the North West African coast.

m.v. TEME

I remember one cold snowy February night we had sailed from Aarhus in eastern Denmark bound south to the Kiel Canal. The Kiel Canal runs roughly north east – south west through northern Germany and is a short cut between the Baltic Sea and North Sea and vice versa. An hour or so after clearing the port of Aarhus we sailed into a horrific snow storm. About three hours later we had to find a specific buoy and then make a 90° turn to starboard to enter the

Samsø Belt, and weave our way down through the Danish islands in the Kattegat. Ordinarily this would not be considered a technically difficult piece of navigation, but on this particular night with gale force winds blowing out of the east, we had blizzard conditions with near zero visibility. It was very much a problem.

CHRISTMAS DAY 1986 IN THE BAY OF BISCAY

Most radars including modern digital daylight radars, do not respond well in snow. Although they can be adjusted to depress a lot of the return clutter, in a bad storm the snow is reflected as interference on the screen. In extreme cases this can block out the screen as a complete whiteout; absolutely nothing shows.

The natural deep-water channel, through which we were sailing, meandered its way through a solid rock sea floor. The buoy, which we were so desperate to find, marked the equivalent of a T-junction with solid rock ahead and on both sides.

In these adverse conditions, and as the ship carried only basic navigational equipment, it was difficult to know for sure exactly where we were in relation to the buoy and gauge the time when we should make our 90° turn. If we turned too early we would hit the rocky bottom on our starboard side, too late and we would run into the rocks which lay ahead and formed the eastern edge of the southbound natural deep-water channel. I was on the bridge along with the 2nd officer (who was the Officer of the Watch) plus the two duty crewmen.

When a ship is at sea, the International Rules for the Prevention of Collision at Sea require that there is a lookout at all times during the hours of darkness or during times of reduced visibility. Consequently the Officer of the Watch also had a lookout with him on the bridge that night plus the helmsman whose job it was to manually steer the ship. Everybody realised the seriousness of our situation and were totally focussed on sighting this buoy. It is a known and accepted fact that sailors the world over always have one hand for themselves then one hand for the ship, so there are times when self interests are high up on their agenda. This was one of them, as no one - myself included - had any interest in becoming another marine casualty statistic or ending up swimming in the freezing waters of the Kattegat!

The basic rule in any difficult navigation situation is always to check, re-check then go back and check again. Knowing what time we cleared the harbour at Aarhus, and having a reasonable idea of the speed we had made, it stood to reason we should be able to calculate at what time we could expect to arrive at the buoy. At least this is the theory because due to the severity of the snowstorm with its accompanying poor visibility we could not regularly check our progress. It is at these times when a navigator might not openly admit it, but the skill of navigation becomes less than an art and more of a guess! Of course there were many unknown imponderables to include in this equation, such as wind and tidal drift etc. As we were all straining our eyes through powerful binoculars, peering into the blinding snow desperately trying to find this small white blinking light, to say I was starting to feel a little anxious was an understatement!

If we could not physically see the buoy and its flashing light, and if we could not see its echo on the radar, the decision, as to when to make the turn, fell solely onto the shoulders of me: the Captain. Putting it bluntly, we were in a bit of a pickle. Some mariners and colleagues I know might well say that this was a 'character building' situation, but it certainly did not feel like it to me at the time. Trying hard to instil confidence in both the Officer of the Watch and two crew members, I went back into the dimly lit chartroom to check the chart yet again and to offer up a small prayer. I was now genuinely worried and concerned, not only for the ship, but also for the lives of all the crew. I never did work out how long anyone could survive in those freezing waters, but I'm sure it would have only been a few minutes.

I was back in the chartroom, checking yet again, when all of a sudden there was a shout "*Sir, quickly come here*". With my heart in my mouth for I had no idea what I was going to find, I rushed out into the darkness of the bridge. There, Miracle of Miracles, the snow had stopped and there - about half a mile off the starboard bow – exactly where it should be was a flashing white light. Trying to appear as calm as I could and keeping my voice level, I asked the 2nd officer whether he had identified the buoy as the one we were looking for. Every navigation buoy, lighthouse and other lighted navigation mark throughout the world, is identifiable by a different sequence of flashes or coloured lights. As we counted the flashing sequence for the third time, identifying the buoy beyond all doubt, the relief for all of us on the bridge was tangible.

As the buoy drew level with our ship's beam, so the course alteration of 90° was made, and we then headed south. Having allowed the ship to settle down onto her new course, the 2nd officer and I went back into the chart room to check the ship's position and make sure all was well. By the time we returned back out to the wheelhouse, the snow blizzard had resumed and visibility was reduced once more to zero. The 2nd Officer and I discussed this miracle and we both agreed it left us with a simple question: "*Is there really a God who hears and answers prayer?*"

We experienced many other interesting incidents aboard the *Teme*, one of which is worthy of mention. Having loaded a full cargo of paper pulp in the Moroccan port of Kénitra, we were bound for Rochester in the River Medway and, after an uneventful passage up the Iberian coast and across the Bay of Biscay, we arrived off Folkestone, on the Kent coast, where we embarked the local pilot for the Medway River. It so happened that I knew the pilot quite well and, as we proceeded through the sheltered waters of the Thames Estuary, we shared lunch on the bridge, chatting about old times and the imminent change in the Pilotage service.

The crew, in preparation for docking at Rochester, were bringing up the mooring ropes that are kept below decks during an ocean passage, when they made a surprising discovery. A stowaway! The Chief Officer and Bosun between them brought this, somewhat bedraggled, specimen onto the bridge. He had brought some food and water with him when he sneaked aboard the ship, but insufficient for almost a week at sea. Stowaways from any country, aboard any ship, are seriously bad news. Most governments do not want the stowaways to land in their country, and consequently have legislated for the ships that have them aboard to pay a hefty fine. It then falls upon the ship owner to be responsible for the safe repatriation of the stowaway, including all travel costs and the provision of security escorts.

I was a bit taken aback at this discovery because, immediately prior to sailing from Kénitra, our Chief Officer should have carried out a thorough routine search of the ship for stowaways. *"I will deal with the Chief Officer later"* I thought, as my mind filled with the prospect of all the paperwork looming ahead. It fleetingly crossed my mind to simply let him go when we had docked, but the pilot had also witnessed the stowaway's arrival onto the ship's bridge, and he too had a responsibility to report it to the authorities before our arrival in port. Considerable problems he may have brought me but he was, after all, another human being and so there was only one thing to do - we gave him a good meal and then he was escorted and securely locked into a locker in the fo'c'sle head. I had no option but to inform the Port Authorities, as well as the ship's owners and their P & I Club (insurers). When we docked later that afternoon the authorities were waiting to meet us! Little sleep was had that night as each representative of the appropriate governmental departments had to have his or her say.

The stevedores worked throughout the night and our cargo was discharged by morning. With all the authorities satisfied, our stowaway ashore and safely in the hands of the Immigration Department, we were ready to sail again on the next tide bound behind the Iron Curtain for the East German port of Wismar. Whilst we were still in the Port of Rochester, I received an official warning from HM Government. It appeared that the East German Authorities were selling food products that had been contaminated by the radioactive fallout from the Chernobyl disaster. Therefore the British Government was warning all British and British Protectorate registered ships not to purchase their ship's stores whilst in the DDR.

In due course I felt confident enough to apply for, sit and pass my DSP licence examination. Having passed, I was, in addition to being a licensed London River Pilot, now also qualified to pilot ships anywhere within the English Channel, Dover Straits and all of the North Sea. In the UK there were, in fact there still are, two separate agencies co-ordinating the use of British Deep Sea Pilots; one is Hammonds, a well-established shipping agency based at Dover. The other, a retired DSP himself, called Hutchings of Gravesend. Upon the death of 'Hutch' as he was universally known, this agency was sold and taken over by a Dutch shipping company. I chose Hammonds of Dover, not only because they are a large well-established and well-known company on the South Coast of England, having many branches and contacts including a shipping agency, but also because I thought they were better equipped, with a good infrastructure to handle all the necessary administration. For the following two years I was gainfully self-employed again, piloting ships throughout these dangerously treacherous but interesting waters.

Working from the end of a telephone at home, you never knew when you were going to be called, where you would be going or how long you would be away. In every DSP's briefcase copies would be found of all the European train timetables as well as flight and ferry timetables. We estimated each pilot travelled around 50,000 miles every year, and that was just getting to and from work!

The life of a DSP was often very unpredictable, even more than his colleague the District Pilot. I had entered and qualified for a county golf tournament, and was preparing to take part in the first day's play when the telephone rang. "*Ah, Captain Wells*" said the agent's clerk on the end of the line, "*We need you to go up to Felixstowe and join a Belgian container ship for just a quick run across to Zeebrugge*". Working out the times and tides, I figured that, if all went well, I could do this job and be back home in time for the start of the golf tournament. So, packing just one clean spare set of clothes, I made my way up to the Suffolk port and duly joined the ship. We sailed from Felixstowe on a balmy summer evening and, as we made our way across the North Sea, the Captain and I were enjoying a general chat with the inevitable cup of coffee, when I happened to mention in passing that I hoped there were not any delays in docking, because I wanted to be back at home the following day as I was due to play in the golf tournament. He looked at me sideways and said: "*Don't you know, we shall only be in Zeebrugge for one full tide and then we are off to Germany and Denmark and you're my DSP*".

I was a very unhappy sailor when I returned home over a week later. I did not get a refund of my tournament entrance fee, and to make matters even worse, I had to go ashore in Zeebrugge to purchase clean clothes!

On another occasion I received orders to travel down to the docks in the Bristol Channel port of Avonmouth. The ship I was to join was a communist Chinese ship called *Ye Ning Hai* bound for the communist East German port of Rostock. After a routine departure from Avonmouth, we disembarked our local pilot and set course to the south west passing inside Lundy Island. Sometime during the middle of the night we rounded Lands End in dense fog. Having safely negotiated Land's End and moving safely clear of all land, we started steaming up the English Channel, after which I went off to bed for a well deserved sleep. It was in the middle of the afternoon when I was woken from a deep sleep by a constant banging on my cabin door. The seaman outside my door was shouting "*the captain needs you on the bridge right now, chop, chop Sar.*" In such circumstances one never asks questions, but throws on some clothes and rushes up to the bridge.

In such circumstances, the first thing any pilot or captain should do on reaching the bridge is to scan the horizon and check the ship's compass to ensure the ship is still on the correct course and that there is nothing close by into which we may crash. All seemed to be well and so I went out onto the starboard bridge wing where it seemed half the crew were gathered. The captain and his political commissar, along with the chief engineer and chief officer were excitedly jabbering away and looking aft to the lifeboat. It seemed we had a stowaway on board. It was obvious that the captain, who spoke only broken English, wanted me both as a witness and an interpreter. The stowaway was literally dragged up to the bridge looking very apprehensive until he saw my occidental face, whereupon he demanded to know, in a rather belligerent manner, what ship he was on, where we were and our destination. This needed strong handling, and with a stern word of authority I reminded him that he was hardly in any position to demand anything, least of all in such an unpleasant way. Recalling the problems experienced with the stowaway when I was in command of the *Teme* in Rochester, it was a comfort to know that this was not my direct responsibility. Eventually our stowaway calmed down when he realised his predicament, and I actually started to feel a little sorry for him. Here he was - a stowaway, aboard a communist Chinese ship, bound for an East German communist port - he could not have picked a worse ship or a worse destination. With some reluctance, I eventually agreed to interview him. It transpired that our unwelcome guest was a registered British able seaman who went ashore in Avonmouth and had had 'one too many'. Returning to the docks he was unable to find his own ship, so he boarded ours.

I had operated on many mainland Chinese ships before and knew that aboard these ships when in port (at least it was the case back in the 1980's), after all the crew were accounted for at the end of the day, the duty officer would ensure that all of the outside doors to the accommodation were locked. Our stowaway, on discovering he could not gain access to the warm accommodation, headed off to the boat deck where he knew he would find shelter and, if necessary, food and water in one of the ship's lifeboats. So, making himself comfortable he had settled down for a good night's sleep. The problem was that by the time he had come out of his drunken stupor, we were far away and steaming up the English Channel. When he finally realised that I was only the westerner aboard this communist Chinese ship bound for the communist East Germany, our stowaway became distinctly contrite. He was given some food then taken away and locked in one of the spare crew cabins with one of the ship's petty officers standing guard. A conference was held in the captain's quarters to which I was invited, or was it perhaps ordered? The discussions revolved around what should or could be done with our uninvited guest. We could divert to either a French or English port, which meant untold delays and red tape, but as we had a tight schedule to keep if we were to reach Rostock on time, any unnecessary delays were simply unacceptable. Then, to my horror and because no one knew this man was aboard, it was actually suggested that he could be disposed of during the night as we sailed through the Dover Straits! The likelihood of any person surviving the strong tides and these cold waters was minimal, and the probability of a body being found unlikely. It was at this point that I stood up and demanded to know whether the commissar was serious with his suggestion. He was! Such was the value the communist Chinese had for human life. Naturally, I wanted no part of this and told the captain that I was going to report the situation to the Dover Coastguard, which caused great consternation to all who were present. I do believe they were all initially taken aback at the vehemence of my outburst.

This problem was finally resolved when I was assured that they were only discussing and examining the options open to them, and that the stowaway would not be thrown over the side. Nevertheless, these people were serious! Our next port of call was to be Brunsbuttel, at the western end of the Kiel Canal, West Germany, where we were to dock and take on fuel before continuing our passage through the canal. It was agreed that when we were docked alongside the oil jetty and during the hours of darkness, the Chinese guards stationed aboard the ship at the top of the gangway would invite the German security guards, who were also aboard the ship and stationed at the top of the gangway, into the crew's mess for a hot cup of coffee. Whilst the gangway was unguarded for that short period, this would be the opportune time for our friend to make his escape. When I relayed this to the stowaway, plus the alternatives that had been proposed, he accepted meekly, without hesitation or question. This was such a complete contrast to his initial attitude when we had first met only a few hours earlier. What was interesting to observe, was the sympathy shown by the ordinary crew members towards our seafaring stowaway, for they were sure he was on the run from the British Authorities. Their sympathies towards this stranger in his apparent attempt to avoid the authorities stemmed from their own first hand knowledge of living in their homeland of China. For having to avoid and keep one step ahead of the authorities was no strange or uncommon experience to them.

He was given some spare warm clothes the Chinese crew had rustled up between them, and I personally gave him 150 Deutsche Marks with the suggestion that if he made it clear of the docks, then he should make his way to the British Consulate in the port of Hamburg and explain his predicament. The ploy worked and he did get away from the ship. I never heard anything further, and I have often wondered what became of him. One thing I am sure of is that I never want to find myself in such a situation again.

In April 1988 I was appointed to a small Korean oil tanker - only 2,800 tons - to pilot her from Brixham in Devon to Rotterdam. Brixham was the major UK shipping and landing port for all DSPs who had ships to take up and down the English Channel and through the Dover Straits into the North Sea and beyond.

I duly arrived by train at Paignton and was met by the car to take me on the final leg to Brixham itself, in ample time before the ship's arrival. Those pilots living far away from Brixham always made it a point to arrive there at least four hours before their ship was due, as this allowed for errors in the ETA and also allowed the pilot to rest up before the long trek eastwards towards the Dover Straits.

The ship was late - which was not uncommon - and so I passed the time wandering around the lovely little fishing port and town of Brixham. Returning to the Tor Bay Shipping Agency's office where DSPs of all European nations gathered, there was still no sign of our ship. After the agency had contacted the British Coastguard informing them of the situation and a possible missing ship, long-range radio messages were sent and eventually radio contact of sorts was made. It transpired that the ship was lost and, having sailed past Brixham, proceeded on her way up the English Channel looking for the pilot station. Eventually directions were sent to the ship to help them find their way back down the Channel to Brixham, where she finally arrived some eighteen hours late. Needless to say, by the time I got on board I was a very unhappy pilot! On most ships of all nationalities there is usually at least one member of the crew who can speak passable English, but that did not seem to be the case here.

The English Channel, Dover Straits and North Sea, like many of the very busy waterways of the world are divided up into shipping lanes, where compliance with both shipping lane regulations and protocol are mandatory. I had noticed, whilst I was aboard, that the charts this ship was carrying were very much out of date and did not show the mandatory routing. The weather forecast for the following morning was for thick dense fog to cover most of the English Channel and Dover Straits, just about where we would be at daybreak, the worst possible time for fog. With this in mind I wanted to make certain what little and basic equipment we had on board was in good working order, but I was experiencing considerable difficulty in trying to convey to the Captain and his officers what it was I wanted. *"Please, will you switch on the main power so I can turn the radar on?!"* It was because of their reluctance to co-operate with my requests that my suspicions were aroused. The Radio Officer finally came to the wheelhouse and with a guilty smile said *"Velly velly sorry meester pilot, I think we have big problem. The radar - it not work".*

Ordinarily fog, no matter how thick and dense it may be, does not cause us too many difficulties provided the radars are in good working order. These two were not and as no sensible Master Mariner, let alone a licensed pilot, would consider taking any ship through the Dover Straits in zero visibility without good navigational equipment, so I turned the ship around and headed back towards Brixham. I thought the poor captain was going to have a fit when I told him that he needed to have a minimum of one radar set in good working condition before we could transit the Straits, and so we were returning to Brixham where repairs could be undertaken.

Great consultations were then had on the bridge between the captain, his officers, and senior engineers and as the pilot boat approached the ship carrying the shore-based electronic service engineer, the captain informed me that he could not wait for repairs and said that if I did not wish to pilot his ship to Rotterdam, then he would do it by himself. Remember that Deep Sea Pilotage was not compulsory and while having a

DSP on board was hugely beneficial, it remained the captain's prerogative as to whether one was employed or not. In spite of my advice - that I did not think it a sensible idea to proceed without repairs - the captain was adamant that he could not wait, so I left the ship only a couple of hours after I had joined it. As we sped back to the shore, the ship turned around and headed eastwards once more in the general direction of Rotterdam.

I managed to catch the last train to London and went home and gave little further thought to that ship. The following morning BBC news carried a story of a collision in the English Channel, just off Beachy Head, between a small oil tanker and a medium sized general cargo ship. Although there was no loss of life or any major pollution, considerable structural damage had been suffered by both ships. You have probably already guessed which small oil tanker it was...

Shipping is routed up and down the English Channel and Dover Straits, and requires that the eastward bound ships stay south towards the French coast and the westward ships to the north, close to the English coast. Our small ship was, in fact, proceeding eastwards on the wrong side of the Channel. This can be likened to driving a car the wrong way up a major motorway. Later at an arbitration court in London, I was asked for my 'expert' advice. The judge, in his summary, advised that all ship masters, especially those in command of ships carrying dangerous cargoes, who were not familiar with the dangers of these treacherous waters, should be urged by their local agents to employ the services of a fully qualified and experienced DSP. And, to our delight, the words he used when referring to DSPs and their agents was "*the UK's premier DSP agency, Hammonds of Dover*".

I relate this story only to illustrate that even in this age of enlightenment, there are still some unscrupulous ship owners who operate on the very fringe of maritime law - ships such as this one and with crews of dubious qualifications and experience - putting at risk not only ships and their cargoes but the lives of their crews as well.

In my last year operating as a Deep Sea Pilot, I was invited by the Elder Brethren at Trinity House responsible for licensing DSPs to join the panel as an examiner. On the examining Boards there was always an active pilot sitting with the Elder Brethren, and I spent many enjoyable hours at Trinity House examining candidates for their licences; to say nothing of the wonderful lunches we enjoyed each day.

Chapter 12

Back to London's River & Port

The 1987 Pilotage Act, many years in the making, came into effect at 0001 hours on 1st October 1988. After 474 years, Trinity House ceased, at the stroke of a pen, to be the licensing authority for local District (port) pilots. This responsibility was taken over by the local Port Authorities to be known as CPA's (Competent Port Authorities). Unfortunately but all too true, this was, very soon after the takeover, to become known throughout the entire British Shipping Industry as 'Incompetent' Port Authorities.

What was the thinking and rationale behind this change in the law? Many of those in power, but not of the Establishment, resented Trinity House and all it stood for. The Pilotage department was in many ways a closed shop, offering opportunities to just a few highly motivated and qualified mariners. Trinity House had and still has many varied areas of responsibility, but its main powerhouse then was the licensing of the majority of all the Commercial Marine Pilots within the UK. The standard they set and maintained was at the highest level.

Many a Master Mariner aspired to become a pilot, but only a few were chosen. Consequently many were deeply disappointed. The unsuccessful candidates either remained at sea or went ashore and into other maritime related professions such as; Port Control Officers, Coast Guard, Harbour Masters, Marine law, Ship and/or Cargo Surveyors, Insurance Adjusters, Lecturers at Nautical Colleges, or were employed as general maritime administrators. The pilot is very definitely high profile within the worldwide shipping industry, and all the pilots I have known enjoyed both the status and responsibility that came with the job. We were frequently seen as overpaid *Prima Donnas* who never seemed to be at work. Since we spent very little time at the office, the only time anyone ever saw us was when we were not doing anything, because when we were at work, we were afloat and well away from the office.

The official political spin put on the reasons for the need to change was "*all Pilotage services within the UK were inefficiently organised and non-cost effective*". The real reasons were quite different.

Historically, London's port includes both estuary and river, and is spread out over many miles. The Port also has different Pilotage districts, for it is considered that the distances involved were too great for any one man to handle all the piloting competently. There was the River District, my patch, extending from Gravesend to London Bridge including the offshoot rivers, docks, river berths and numerous buoy berths. The 'Downies' were the East Bound pilots based at Gravesend, who took ships out to the sea through both the north and south channels. The North Channel pilots, based at Harwich brought ships into London from the North and East, boarding (although the proper term is 'shipping the pilot') and landing at a position about 12 miles eastward off Harwich harbour known as the 'Sunk'. The South Channel pilots, sometimes known as Cinque Port pilots, brought ships into London arriving from the south. They were based, until 1988, at Folkestone, thereafter at Margate. The system might not have been 100% perfect (what system is?), but it worked and it worked well!

Prior to October 1988 when all pilots were self-employed, the London River pilots would work on average 18 days (or tides) each month, making their own way to and from each berth anywhere within their District, and earnings generated only from those ships they handled. From 1st October 1988, the London River pilots were employees of the Port of London Authority, now paid a salary whether they worked or not. As loving and caring employers who supposedly had the pilots' best interests at heart, transport was provided, at any time of day or night, to take the pilots to and from wherever they were needed. Let me say that in all my years at sea, and this includes seeing action in Biafra and sailing through two full-blown hurricanes, the scariest part of my career was when I was being driven around the London Docks at night by some contracted driver!

GRAVESEND'S PILOT STATION

Since October 1988 the London River Pilots' no longer work their average 18 days each month, but only 6 days, that's right - six days each month! And we had been deemed non cost effective?! Control and costs were certainly two of the main reasons for change. The government authorities never had any real control over the pilots throughout the land. The law states that every commercial ship over a certain size, when entering and leaving a 'compulsory Pilotage' port must have a licensed pilot aboard. If, for example, all the pilots decided to take the day off and have a pilots' picnic somewhere, nobody could stop them because they were all self employed. And so the Country's economy would then be affected for at least one tide as there would be no pilots available; they would be returning from their picnic or wherever they had been. As the vast majority of all pilots in the UK are not of that persuasion, this situation never arose; but this was a 'loose-end' which could have been exploited.

On 1st October 1988, a good number of pilots throughout the land, who had been licensed and therefore self-employed for many years, refused to become employees of the newly formed Competent Port Authorities. They retired or simply went off and did other things. There was a mood throughout the Pilotage Service in the United Kingdom that the pilots had been 'sold short', and the administration of our service, known worldwide for its professionalism, expertise and traditions, had been taken away and given to general business administrators and managers. There are so many imponderables to take into account when running a Pilotage service and these very same administrators and managers demonstrated quickly just how little knowledge they had of how an efficient Pilotage service worked.

Adverse weather does not have to be experienced in the port to cause delays - many a ship is delayed when arriving at the pilot station, because adverse weather or poor visibility has been experienced out in the English Channel and North Sea or even further afield. Ships are not affected by weather alone - there are also the tides to take into account, as well as a host of potential mechanical failures just waiting to happen. Ships' movements can also be very unpredictable and it took several years for one manager to understand that, although a ship might be travelling along at say 10 knots and having 10 miles to go to the berth or pilot station, it does not necessarily mean that it will take 1 hour! The days of October, November and December 1988 were totally chaotic, especially in the Port of

London, although equally shambolic in other ports as well. For many of the disappointed and frustrated 'would be' pilots who never made the grade, this was payback time. There were and indeed still are, many harbour masters and marine administrators whose office took over the Pilotage Service within their port, who deliberately went out of their way to try to make the life of their District pilots difficult. This has been illustrated in several high profile incidents which have occurred since 1988 within, what had hitherto been, 'compulsory Pilotage' ports. For example there has been the liberal allocation of PEC's (pilot exemption certificates - see below) to those mariners who ordinarily would not be qualified to hold such a certificate.

Considerable pressure has also been applied to relatively inexperienced pilots, in the absence, for whatever reason, of their more senior colleagues to undertake 'acts of Pilotage' for which their pilot's licence does not qualify them. This has resulted in national disasters which go far beyond a mere 'shipping' incident by causing widespread pollution of our coastlines. And the list continues to go on and on.

The Government, with the support of many independent ship owners, got what they wanted; the power of Trinity House was lessened and the number of licensed and apparently expensive pilots reduced. Everybody involved with the movement of ships within British ports agreed that the system we had in place prior to October 1988 may not have been perfect, but when any ship ordered a pilot, she got one...and at the time the pilot was ordered for! It was always considered unforgivable, pre October 1988, for a pilot to be late in joining a ship, no matter what the circumstances were. Certainly within the Port of London, it rapidly became the norm for ships to be delayed, because of the lack of pilots available, and in worst-case scenarios ships were even given permission by the Harbour Master to sail without a pilot.

In the eyes of the authorities it was assumed that all captains who were regular callers into British ports would take a Pilot Exemption Certificate (PEC), thus obviating the need and cost of employing a professionally licensed pilot. A 'PEC ' was a certificate granted to a ship's master by the competent port authority, exempting him from using the services of an authorised/licensed pilot, thus allowing him to bring a specified named ship into and out from a specified named berth or dock in the specified port. Many of the questionable shipping companies and their port agents used and abused this system, to the extent that the authorities were finally forced to re-evaluate it.

The forced introduction of a 'PEC' system clearly indicated, yet again, the lack of knowledge and understanding of the psyche of seafaring master mariners and ships' captains, by those brought in to run the Pilotage services. Firstly, aboard many of the smaller ships with correspondingly smaller crews, frequently the only respite the captain had, especially during the winter months when sailing through bad weather, was when the pilot came aboard. There were many ships' captains who greeted the pilot with the words, "*good to have you aboard pilot, perhaps I can now go and get some rest. Please call me just before we arrive at our berth*". And he would go away and get his much needed rest, comfortable in the knowledge his ship was in the hands of a competent professional.

Secondly, the majority of shipmasters did not actually want to have to do the piloting themselves, so they were very happy for a licensed pilot to be aboard. Yet many of these captains, who had given countless years of loyal service to their ship owners, were forced to do so under the threat of being replaced by someone else who would be willing to take on more responsibility; usually someone from an emerging nation. To cap it all, there was many a captain who vociferously complained that, although his employers were willing to pay them to pilot their own ship, the amount of fee offered was so derisory it was insulting. These were very difficult days throughout the UK Pilotage services. Whether one likes it or not, nothing ever stays the same, and so over a period of several months leading into years, a pattern developed under the new regime and we all, eventually, settled into the new working structures, albeit with a certain degree of reluctance. I am sure that the 'Competent' Port Authorities who employ pilots would deny this but I, and many of my colleagues agree that, following the changes which have been introduced into the UK Pilotage services since 1988, the general administration as well as the overall standards of professionalism, service and attitude of many of the new intake of pilots, has steadily deteriorated.

Not willing to heed the advice of their pilots, who between them had literally centuries of experience, the Port of London Authority did, a few years post 1988 finally acknowledge they had got their sums wrong, especially with regards to forward planning. They realised that their expectation of the number of ships' captains who were willing to perform their own Pilotage was badly miscalculated. Ignoring the fact that it takes approximately five years for every new pilot to become a 'class 1 pilot', that is when he can finally operate without any restrictions as to the size of ships he is cleared to handle, increasingly more experienced pilots were taking early retirement. In the Port of London, on pure financial grounds, recruitment of new pilots had all but dried up, and then suddenly the numbers showed at least twelve new pilots were needed each year and for the foreseeable future, just to maintain the status quo. I am sure that, in the 474 years in which Trinity House was responsible for pilots operating on the London River and Estuary, there was never such a shortage.

To us 'Old Hands' another travesty occurred when the PLA decided, in their wisdom, that there was a need for the river and estuary pilots to overlap. For countless years the London sea (estuary) pilots brought the ships in from the sea and handed over their charges to the river pilot at Gravesend. Outward bound the river pilot handed back over to the sea pilot who then took the ship back out to sea. This was a straightforward system which everyone involved with ships in the Port knew and understood - the ship owner, ship's captain, ship's agents, tug companies, ship movement co-ordinators, lightermen, boatmen, stevedores, customs and excise. Before we knew it we were training sea pilots to take over our work, from Gravesend eight miles up river to Crayfordness. At the same time we river pilots were retraining to bring ships in from the Nore to Gravesend and then continue up river. The majority of the sea pilots and river pilots did not welcome this enforced decision. Who says politics make sense?

The Nore is the official eastern extremity of the actual River Thames, south east of Shoeburyness in Essex. This area was made famous when, in 1797, the crews of the entire Royal Navy Fleet who were anchored there, mutinied.

In spite of continually being confronted with a wide range of new problems almost daily, we continued to enjoy and have a lot of fun when handling all the different types and sizes of ships calling into our port. We have already seen that there are a lot more strings to the District Pilot's bow than just a safe passage and the safe handling of ships. In addition to those two fundamental skills, the pilot is also a fount of local knowledge and in a wider sense, au fait with all customs and regulations that are required for incoming foreign ships. He must be a diplomat even in times of high tension and pressure, as well as being capable of demonstrating an understanding of the customs of those from a different culture. For example, there is little to be gained if, on a ship manned by personnel from the Far East, one starts to bark out orders in a brusque manner. In their culture, the recipient, whoever he may be, would 'lose face' and the pilot would then be confronted with an extremely difficult situation that, in all probability, would be irrecoverable. After many years experience of exposure to ships and their personnel who come from other nations and cultures, one gains a good idea of what to expect. We would encounter the grateful and generous Greek, at last getting a pilot aboard to guide his ship into port (I always felt a bit uncomfortable when receiving a 'docking gift', usually cigarettes or a bottle of Black Label, before I had actually docked or berthed his ship, it was a bit like tempting fate), the excitable Italian, unflappable Scandinavian, efficient German, indifferent Russian, know-it-all Dutchman or American and so on.

Most experienced pilots and ships' captains, when faced with an increasingly pressurised situation, fight to keep their voices to a low and flat monotone. I include myself in this context, having worked hard over the years to perfect this control. Working on the basis that, no matter what the situation is, or how much one's stomach may be churning, if calmness and control are seen to be the order of the day then subordinates will follow that lead. I am sure that many of my experienced colleagues will have joined me as I always gave a wry smile when hearing, on the ship to ship radio, a rise in octaves in the voice of an inexperienced or unsure pilot, as things start to go wrong (as they sometimes do) and he struggles to communicate with his tugs or boatmen, and risks losing control of the situation.

A major advancement in ship handling came about towards the end of the 1970's, when both increases in port charges and general manning reductions started to bite. Ship owners started to have forward thrusters and occasionally stern thrusters built into their ships to avoid the high costs of having to employ the use of tug boats. Controls for these thrusters, main ship's engines and steering points were all duplicated on both sides of the ship's bridge wings, in addition to the master system sited inside the wheelhouse. This was often a double-edged sword, as it gave some captains a confidence in ship handling they had never before experienced. However, inevitably, a growing number of captains started to think they were more capable of handling their ship than was the local pilot and while, in very few cases this may have been true, generally speaking, when manoeuvring in confined tidal waters, there is never a substitute for local knowledge and experience.

The Panama Canal is a benchmark for many of the world's tidal ports which require locks that lead into their enclosed docks, either from the open sea or rivers. From this benchmark evolved and developed the Panamax sized ship, i.e. the maximum size ship, which can transit the Panama Canal. This measurement is not based on tonnage, length or draught, but on the beam, or width of the ship. Roughly speaking the width of all the locks within the Panama Canal is 108 feet. The maximum width of any ship permitted to transit the canal is 106 feet.

The locks leading into Tilbury Dock, situated at the lower end of the River Thames, measure 1000 feet long by 108 feet wide. London river pilots do regularly put a Panamax sized ship measuring up to 850 feet in length by 106 feet wide into this lock giving only one foot clearance on each side, so there was little room for error. On a good day, with a fair wind, we prided ourselves that we could slide the ship into the lock without even touching the sides; on a bad day...well let's not go there, shall we?!

One day during the Spring Tide (that is when the tides are at their highest and tidal flow [current] is at its strongest), and the prevailing sou'westerly wind was blowing quite hard, accompanied by two 'tripping' pilots I boarded a large high-sided Panamax size Italian ship, bound for the Tilbury Dock. Approaching the lock entrance with such strong wind and swirling currents called for absolute total concentration. Three tugs were secured to the ship to assist in the manoeuvre and we were all out on the port wing of the bridge as the ship approached the entrance to the lock. To be fair, the view one gets from the wheelhouse and bridge wing is a bit daunting to say the least. When seen from high above the river, the entrance really does look too narrow for the ship to fit into. The Italian captain, who was new to that particular ship and had never been into Tilbury Dock before, was very clearly of a nervous disposition and visibly apprehensive. My comforting words of "*trust me captain, I'm a pilot and have done this manoeuvre countless times*" did nothing to help him relax.

PANAMAX SHIP IN TILBURY LOCK

With the ship angled across the entrance to the lock to counter the increasingly strong wind, and as the narrow entrance of the lock approached nearer and nearer, I noticed the ship was not responding as I expected her to. On checking by radio with the tugs, I was assured they were doing exactly as I had ordered and yet the ship was still unresponsive. The vast majority of all manoeuvres do proceed as anticipated, but there is invariably the occasion when a planned manoeuvre throws in a surprise and the ship seems to have a mind of her own. Even the most experienced pilots, although always prepared for this, do not like it when it actually happens.

AND IT WASN'T ME!

In the adverse weather and tidal conditions we were experiencing that day, my idea was to bring the ship up to a position just before the lock entrance, then stop her completely. The wind and tide would then blow the ship gently alongside the landing pier that had been designed precisely for that purpose. Having landed alongside the pier, the ship is then 'knuckled' around the corner and then worked up into the lock proper. This always looks a lot more difficult than it really is, and this day was no exception.

The problem was that the ship's bow kept falling away to the other side of the lock entrance that consisted of very hard and solid granite. For the life of me I couldn't fathom out why this was happening - not until one of the qualifying pilots drew my attention to the captain, who was surreptitiously using the bow thruster to keep the ship off the fenders. It was this action that was causing the ship's bow to fall off to the other side of the lock entrance. As the opening loomed ever closer, the situation was becoming increasingly critical. Now aware of what was happening, my reflex reaction, without thinking, was to smack the captain's hand away from the thruster controls and bring the ship back under control. Having later apologised to the captain, explaining why it is necessary to go so close to the lock wall, I believed that was the end of the matter. But oh no, the two pilots who were aboard observing regaled this incident, not only to our colleagues at all the London Pilot Stations, but later to their pilot friends who operated in other ports as well. Once again, infamy had caught up with me! That particular captain not only became a regular visitor to Tilbury but we became friends as well and shared many a good laugh over that incident.

VIEW APPROACHING TILBURY LOCK

8th July 1989 saw the last Tall Ships' Race start out from the Pool of London. What a fantastic sight was the Upper Pool of London: there were sailing ships from every maritime nation - large square riggers, small ships, tall ships, you name it and they were present. What a day that was and, I think, each and every river pilot would have worked for free if necessary, not only for the sheer professional pleasure of seeing these great ships from yesteryear, but also of playing an active part in their movements on the river that one day.

PILOT AT WORK

As a one-off occasion, we river pilots decided to draw straws to see which of these magnificent ships each of us would bring down the river. I found myself detailed to be the pilot aboard the Portuguese schooner *Creole* which was berthed alongside *HMS Belfast* and heading up river. With an audience of several thousand, the ship had to be turned through 180° with the aid of tugs between London Bridge and Tower Bridge, before proceeding down river, 'dressed' from bow to stern. When a ship is 'dressed' it means she has flags hoisted from the bow to the top of the mast, and if she has two masts, flags hoisted between the two and then from the second or main mast back down to the stern. When a sailing ship is 'dressed' it means her crew will man the rigging of each mast, on both sides of the ship; a spectacular sight. This was a fantastically fabulous day enjoyed by an estimated audience of three million people, on both sides of the river, all the way from London Bridge to the Thames Barrier.

PORTGUESE SCHOONER CREOLE

18th June, 1992, I was detailed to join *HMS London*, a Type 22 frigate of the Royal Navy anchored off Southend Pier and inbound for *HMS Belfast. HMS London* was originally named *HMS Bloodhound* but was renamed at the specific request of the Lord Mayor of London. She was the flagship of the Royal Navy during the First Gulf War and sold to the Romanian Navy in 2003, being renamed *Regina Maria* in 2005 after an extensive refit.

As we approached Woolwich and prior to passing through the Thames Barrier we embarked Sir Brian Jenkins, then the Lord Mayor of London, who had expressed a wish to travel aboard *HMS London* and pass through both the Thames Barrier and Tower Bridge into central London. He had his wish granted on a wonderful hot summer day!

1993 witnessed the British Sailors' Society - an international Christian based organisation dedicated to the welfare of seamen from all nations - celebrate its 175th anniversary. As the British Sailors' Society was partially responsible for providing my scholarship and subsequent first trip to the UK way back in the beginning of 1957 (as mentioned in Chapter 1) I had always kept in contact with them, and they, in turn, kept an eye on my career.

The celebrations were to be on a grand scale. HM Queen Elizabeth 2nd is the Society's Patron so she was the natural figure to head up the celebrations. BBC television had decided to use these celebrations in one of their Sunday night productions, "Songs of Praise". I never did find out who, but someone decided it would be a good idea to film me whilst I was piloting a ship on the River. It so happened that there was a small cruise ship moored just below Tower Bridge, and she was scheduled to sail on a day and time suitable to all parties concerned. The TV crew, Head of Public Relations of the Port of London and myself as the operating pilot, all boarded *m.v. Song of Flower* on the afternoon of 23rd June 1993 for the passage downriver to Gravesend. After backing the ship down river for over a mile I turned her around to head the right way, then the host of the programme, Pam Rhodes, started interviewing me. It was now that I was about to learn a lesson I have never forgotten. No matter who you are, you must be so, so very careful what you say when speaking to ANYONE from any form of the media.

As we sailed down river and the interview progressed, I was asked among many things, "*Is being a pilot and 'driving' ships a boy's own dream?*" To which I replied: "*In my opinion, definitely yes*". When viewing the actual TV programme that part was shown verbatim. However, another section, which was taken completely out of context, showed me saying on national TV to an estimated audience of over four million people: "*Pilots are basically glorified parking attendants*". You can imagine how well that was received by my colleagues!

A few days later I received an invitation to join a selected audience on the docks at Southampton, where the BBC would be filming the songs and hymns sung in the presence of Her Majesty the Queen and HRH Duke of Edinburgh. That was another great and memorable occasion, one more certainly to put in the memory banks.

1993 proved to be an eventful year as there was yet another event which I shall never forget.

Sitting at home off duty on the evening of 14th July 1993, the telephone rang and the Duty Pilot asked if I was available for an overtime job, to bring a German small bulk carrier, *m.v. Barbel* downriver. With nothing better to do that night, plus the thought of an overtime payment, I agreed.

Upon arrival at the berth it was apparent the discharge of cargo had not been completed and there would be a delay in sailing. The German captain was very apologetic and offered coffee which was brought to me on the ship's bridge by some nondescript crew member. The captain having made his apologies then left me to my own devices whilst he went off to supervise the preparation of his ship for sea.

We finally sailed about 40 minutes later than anticipated and had an uneventful passage down the 9 miles of river before I handed the ship over to the sea-pilot who relieved me at Gravesend for the passage out into the estuary. After calling into the office to complete my paperwork, I went home and thought nothing more about it.

Later that week I received a telephone call from the local constabulary, asking if I would be available at home to receive a member of Interpol who was coming down from London and wished to speak to me. Needless to say my guilt ridden mind was in a whirl as I wracked my brains to recall anything I may have said or done which warranted a visit from such an esteemed body!

The appointed day arrived and two 'plain clothes' gentlemen knocked on my front door and after inviting them into my home, the first thing they insisted on was to see my pilot's identification and I their police ID's. With those formalities completed I was then questioned about the ship I had brought down the river on the previous Saturday evening. An experienced pilot can quickly ascertain the atmosphere aboard any ship and I was asked if I had detected any atmosphere of hostility on the *Barbel*. Had I overheard arguments amongst the crew? Who brought me my coffee to the bridge, could I recognise him from a book of 'mug shots' of the entire crew they had with them. The answers to most of their questions were all negative; as I explained for the umpteenth time, that this had been a 'run-of-the mill' operation, and there was nothing exceptional which came to mind including the unexpected delay in sailing.

It transpired the ship had been found abandoned on the Monday morning out in the North Sea. When the German authorities boarded, they found eight of the nine crew members dead, all mutilated, blood splattered everywhere with the ship's safe empty having been forced open and evidence of attempts to set the ship on fire.

A few days later the lifeboat bearing the name of the ship landed on the West coast of Denmark manned by one seaman carrying several thousand pounds worth of foreign currencies and wearing a Rolex watch which was later identified as the captain's by his widow who had given it to him as a present several years earlier. Needless to say the said seaman was arrested and extradited to Germany where he stood trial for piracy and murder.

As the second to last person to leave the ship (the relieving sea pilot being the last) the police were interested in our assessments and impressions of the ship's atmosphere.

Several weeks later both the sea pilot and I were summonsed across to Ösnabrück in North West Germany where a high profile case was opened to both public and press, including TV cameras. We both appeared in court giving our own account of the time we were aboard and flew back to London the following day.

Two weeks later I received a note of thanks from the German court for my contribution and at the same time informing me of the verdict. The sailor, a Russian national, was found guilty on all counts of murdering 8 people for which he received 8 life sentences. Other custodial sentences were handed down for various other offences he had been charged with.

There was a footnote to this note of thanks which I thought was a bit of an over statement, it read: *"under German law he would never see freedom again!"*

Swan Hellenic's educational cruise ship *Minerva 11* was the largest ship ever to visit London's Upper Pool, and I was detailed to take her up river. Because of her size she had to be turned around beside the infamous Dome, now known as O2, on the Greenwich Peninsular. We went stern first (backwards) for over a distance of five miles. Not for the faint hearted!

m.v. MINERVA 11

Another interesting operation with which I was involved, was The London Eye, the large Ferris type wheel on the South Bank sponsored by British Airways. Barges containing various parts for the Wheel were towed by a tug and brought up-river to a holding point, just below Woolwich, until the tidal conditions allowed the remainder of the passage to be completed. Each trip, and there were many, required the services of a pilot.

The job of taking Mr Grundy's super yacht from Tilbury into the old London Dock just below Tower Bridge was another interesting one. This was the Mr Grundy of Grundy Television studios in Australia, producer of Neighbours and other well-known TV programmes. Mr Grundy himself was aboard for the passage up river from Tilbury. As we approached the Thames Barrier at Woolwich he appeared on the yacht's bridge and introduced himself. Here was a man to whom I took an instant liking, not only because of his overall attitude to life but he was also inquisitive and displayed a genuine interest in all that was going on around him. For the remainder of our passage up-river he questioned me not only about our Pilotage service but the River Thames and her history, and the purpose and practicality of the Thames Barrier.

Over the years I have handled quite a few of the 'Super Luxury' type yachts. I cannot recall ever being aboard one that was designed for easy manoeuvring in confined waters, and this one was no exception. But after a successful passage up river, and having finally eased his yacht into the lock without touching the paintwork on its sides, I was surprised as I was about to disembark to be offered an envelope by the captain. It contained £250 in £50 notes. This was a 'tip' for not damaging the yacht! How I wish all successful berthings and dockings I have performed in my career resulted in such a reward!

On the day of the Twin Towers attack in New York, that fateful day the world will never forget, 11th September 2001, I was sitting at home waiting for the office to call me, as I was to board and pilot an inward German warship, *FGS Elbe*, bound for the West India Docks. A good friend of mine telephoned me asking if I had heard the news. I turned on the television and, like everybody who saw the events unfold live, I could not believe what was happening. On boarding my designated ship later that afternoon when she arrived off the Pilot's Station at Gravesend, the German captain was concerned to get as much information as I could give him, not only about the attack but also on what security measures had been put into place in our Port.

I reassured him that every possible security measure was being taken and that we should continue to proceed up river, making any decision as to whether or not we should enter an enclosed dock later when we were up off the lock. As it happened, the decision was taken out of our hands because the British government immediately decided to halt all aircraft whose flight paths took them over central London and at the same time they closed the upper river and docks to all shipping. As we approached Dagenham, we were ordered to turn around and proceed back down river and out to sea where the captain obviously felt that much safer.

The effects of 9/11 reverberated around the world and we, in the Port of London, were not immune. Overnight we were all forced to become much more security conscious, and access to many of the 'sensitive' parts of the Port was severely restricted, even to those pilots who needed to be there.

For almost 36 years I served in the Pilotage Service. Of the hundreds of pilots I have met, worked with, trained, examined and known socially, I think it safe to say that the majority of them, particularly the old hands who were licensed before 1988, never joined the Service for the money. Pilotage was for us, no matter which port or stretch of sea we operated, more a way of life than it was a job. The money came as a consequence of the work we did. I'm sure I speak for many when I say that what we really loved about being a pilot was not only the technical work, or boarding so many different ships and meeting all kinds of multinational characters, but the status and the lifestyle it afforded us, as well as the responsibility and the authority which accompanied it all.

Imagine this scenario: Central London and it's 5 o'clock on a Friday evening, rush hour, with everybody trying to get home for the weekend. I am bringing a large ship up the river on the tide and we need to pass through Tower Bridge to berth alongside *HMS Belfast.* I speak to the control room of Tower Bridge on my VHF radio informing them of my ETA (Estimated Time of Arrival) at the Bridge, whilst at the same time requesting clearance to proceed up and through the Bridge. Clearance is given and, as I approach the Bridge, the two bascules start to rise. As we transit the Bridge, heading forwards or backwards - it really doesn't make that much difference to the pilot which direction we go - I cannot help noticing, with some glee, as we pass through the Bridge itself, that - as far as the eye can see along Tower Bridge Road - there is total chaos. Cars, buses, lorries, bikes, people are all milling around waiting for us to pass clear and for the Bridge to reopen. There is a major traffic jam, and in fact this part of London and the City is now totally gridlocked. Who caused this? Why, it was Billy Wells from Wellington, New Zealand.

2001 saw me re-married and, to my amazement, not only did my career, but my outlook on life take on a completely different dimension as well; gone was all the single minded dedication, for now I finally realised there was more to life than 'playing' with ships on the river.

Then the day came that I never envisaged would ever arrive; the day I informed the Port Authority that I was intending to retire. After almost 49 continuous years of sea service, including the Pilotage service, my career was coming to its conclusion. And to my astonishment I was ready, for it seemed a life's cycle was about to be completed. When I was asked to say a few words at my farewell presentation, I brought to mind some words of wisdom given to me many years earlier when I was just setting out on my piloting career: "*Try and leave the service you are now entering, a better service than it is today*". In all honesty I couldn't say those words. The service to which I had devoted almost 36 years of my life was, most definitely, not as good, efficient or cost effective as it had been pre 1988. Probably worst of all, I had never known the morale of so many of the pilots nationwide as low as it was in 2005.

As the Cold War came to a close and corresponding military cut backs evolved, many Ports and Pilotage services in England were ambushed by retired naval officers, and the Port of London was no exception. Today, throughout the entire Country, there are more retired ex-naval officers running our ports than ever before but, in general, very few have any practical experience of handling ships or of running a Pilotage service. This transformation is not restricted to these services alone, for there are many other marine services, which had traditionally been run by commercially minded Master Mariners, and are now mainly run by ex naval officers; one might go so far as to say 'a job for the boys!' The future for Master Mariners and professional seamen, from what is left of the British Merchant Navy, does not, in my view, look promising.

Perhaps it is only a fortunate few who have experienced and enjoyed a productive and exciting life, who loved what they had chosen to do and who never look forward to retirement - I must have been one of those, for I never thought of retirement until one day there it was right in front of me. Like everything in life, there is a cycle that catches up with you. And whether I liked it or not, so it did with me. I am reminded of those words from the Biblical book of Ecclesiastes, chapter 3: "*There is a Time for Everything*".

At the end of my long seafaring life, there was to be one last event, which came quite unexpectedly. Upon retirement, I was promoted to the Flag Rank of Commodore. For me, this was the jewel in the crown.

The average pilot, despite the sometimes swaggering exterior, is very much capable of such feelings as love, affection, intimacy and caring. These feelings just don't involve anybody else.

HAPPY PILOT

Chapter 13

Post Career, Career

Without any doubt in the first few weeks and months of my retirement the hardest thing I had to come to terms with was having the luxury of a full night's sleep. Not only did I go to my own bed every night, but the telephone wasn't going to ring at 2, 3 or 4 o'clock. And another issue both my wife and I had to face was the question of how were my days going to be filled, because even I could not play golf every day!

A few years prior to retirement I had become interested in speaking about 'matters maritime' and, with the help of my wordsmith wife, we - or probably more accurately she - put together some talks, which I was able to present to anyone who would listen! Many of the early talks were given for free for not only was I seeking exposure as a speaker, but I also needed the experience of standing up in front of a large audience, hopefully both entertaining and informing them at the same time.

NOW A SPEAKER

Much to our surprise my new post career, career, took off in a way that neither of us could ever have imagined. Fortunately, whilst still in full time employment, the six days or so each month I was on duty allowed me considerable freedom to accept speaking engagements both day and night therefore in the twelve months before I actually retired I was speaking far more than I was piloting. There is that old saying: "*when one door closes so another opens*" and so it did for me. Having retired from my seafaring career, I became virtually a full time public speaker overnight, speaking not of mice and men but of ships and the sea.

As I could see a promising future in this, I decided to put my speaking status on a more formal basis. I became involved with both the Professional Speakers Association and Toastmasters International. Toastmasters International is not to be confused with those men and women who attend formal functions, dressed immaculately in their red coats. Toastmasters International helps and teaches people how to speak in public, the Professional Speakers Association does not. The PSA is a forum for speakers who speak for a living, and helps its members to learn how to set up a speaking business. I was encouraged to attend one of the PSA sponsored Boot Camps for would-be speakers, and this proved to be the best money I have ever invested in myself. I learned more in that one long residential weekend than I did in the first six months of actual speaking.

Today I am fortunate enough to have a large portfolio of contacts, and I speak before a wide range of different organisations including on board cruise ships as well as on BBC local and national radio. Probably the highest accolade I have received so far as a speaker was in 2008, when the Cunard Line invited me to be their Principal Guest Lecturer aboard the final cruise of the world famous *QE2*, immediately prior to her delivery passage to Dubai. I flew to Athens and joined the ship halfway through her cruise in the port of Piraeus, where we sailed that night to a rapturous departure from a large crowd on the quay. Although whilst I was aboard, we only called at Gibraltar, Vigo in northern Spain and then back to her home port of Southampton, at each sailing and arrival hundreds of people came to watch this icon move in and out of their port for the last time. There was an ample supply of small Union Flags on board for any passenger who wanted them to take and wave to people on the shores. Today the *QE2* languishes in Dubai where she is currently undergoing a major conversion to become a floating hotel and tourist attraction. I feel it is such a pity that a similar use could not have been found for the ship somewhere here in these British Islands.

To a lot people, being a speaker aboard a cruise ship, with the accompanying free cruise for both speaker and spouse, sounds an ideal way to spend one's retirement. Many shipping companies expect their speakers to be seen circulating among passengers at the various cocktail parties and in some instances, to 'host' a different table at the numerous 'black-tie' dinners. To me it is always pleasing, the number of passengers who approach me to just pass the time of day or ask questions about my lectures, when I am either walking the decks or relaxing in a deck chair next to my wife. Like most cruise-ship speakers, I am always available to give of my time. There will be times when the speaker will be invited to partake in that old favourite party game we know as "Call My Bluff" or as the Americans would say "Liars Club". And then in certain cases, the speaker will be asked if he or she could help out by acting as an escort to those passengers going ashore on organised excursions. All these extras go with the job.

In the event of giving a 'bad performance' when speaking ashore, the client simply would not recommend you or invite you back again, which in itself is bad enough. Aboard cruise ships the speakers invariably become high profile as part of the entertainment team and in order for all the passengers on board to be aware of what entertainment is available, the Cruise Director will promote and advertise both the lecturers and their lectures, throughout the ship at all times. So if you happen to have a 'bad day' whilst on the high seas, believe me, there is nowhere to run or hide, as everybody on board knows who you are!

My wife and I have now set in place a consultancy in conjunction with some leading cruise companies to help, guide and advise those would-be cruise ship speakers and their partners about what to expect when speaking afloat, what is expected of them and many pitfalls waiting for the uninformed.

Currently I speak aboard 3 or 4 cruise ships each year, and my wife invariably accompanies me when I go back to sea. Most shipping lines look after their guest speakers very well, with both of us enjoying full passenger status with an ocean view stateroom.

I love going back to sea – especially in the knowledge I can now sleep all through the night without being 'called out'. The only negative feelings I have about being aboard cruise ships is the amount of food I see wasted on a daily basis. Accepting all meals are paid for in the ticket price and therefore one can eat as much as one likes, there are times when a definite element of unnecessary greed is evident. As the majority of the dining room staff are people from the third world and what was the Eastern block coming from poor backgrounds, it must be galling for them to have to clear up and dump the food wasted by those passengers who take as much as they can, pile up their plates and then leave most of it. The food I have seen wasted from just one sitting and one table might be sufficient to feed (for a week) the entire family of a crewmember. Even after all these years, I still cannot rid myself of the image of that Indian whom I witnessed being stabbed and dying on the streets of Visakhapatnam, for a simple piece of chapatti bread.

My opportunity to first speak aboard cruise ships, like many things in life, came about quite by chance. I was piloting an elite cruise ship belonging to Seabourn Luxury Yachts from central London to Gravesend. The ship was a regular caller at London during the summer months and I knew the Captain quite well. In the general course of conversation he asked me how my new speaking career was developing. I told him that it was looking encouraging, and he suggested that I should join his ship as a lecturer as they were often short of one. My 'off the cuff' response did much to change our lives. I responded by saying, "*that sounds like a good idea, why not go ahead and organise it*". Thinking nothing more about it we continued down river where I disembarked at Gravesend, having handed the ship over to the Estuary Pilot.

A few days later an email arrived from Miami, inviting me to join the *m.v. Seabourn Pride* as the onboard Enrichment Lecturer the next time she sailed from London on a cruise to the Baltic Sea and the Russian port of St. Petersburg. Admittedly at first I was a bit apprehensive and tempted to decline, but a quick re-arrangement of my leave schedule allowed my wife and I to join this 6 star luxury cruise ship for a 12 day cruise, visiting most of the Baltic capital cities. We joined the ship at *HMS Belfast* and, as we sailed down the River, I was the operational River Pilot. On reaching Gravesend, instead of disembarking the ship as usual, I left the bridge and went down below to our suite and changed out of uniform. For the following 12 days I lectured each day the ship was at sea.

On our return to London when the estuary pilot had brought the ship to Gravesend, I returned to the bridge – now the inward operating pilot - navigating back up river to our berth alongside *HMS Belfast*. As these ships only carry just over 200 passengers, by the time we had returned to London everyone knew everyone else, and they all knew I was the pilot who brought the ship down and who would also be taking her back up the River Thames. This turned out to be very good PR both for me as a fledgling speaker and the shipping company as well. My wife and I sailed aboard that ship for three consecutive years, and we enjoyed every moment visiting and enjoying various different ports and cities.

Today I am in the enviable position of being able to be selective in which cruises I accept. My wife and I should we so choose, could easily spend six to eight months each year at sea aboard different cruise ships. However, I am not sure whether her enthusiasm for going to sea is quite the same as mine!! But I'm also glad that she is a good sailor and is able to accompany me on these cruises, visiting many of the ports I knew when I was at sea.

At the time of writing this 2nd edition of my book, my wife and I have sailed, and I have lectured aboard cruise ships belonging to Silversea Cruises, Seabourn Luxury Yachts, The Cunard Line, Fred Olsen Line, Princess Cruises and Saga Shipping. We have travelled across the Atlantic several times visiting places such as The Faeroe Islands, Iceland, Greenland, United States and Canada. We have also visited Morocco, Canary Islands, Madeira, the Azores, Bermuda, Bahamas, the West Indies and Caribbean. We have sailed down through the Chilean Fjords and Straits of Magellan, across to the Falkland Islands, Argentina, Uruguay and Brazil. We then called into the penal colony known as Devil's Island in French Guiana where we witnessed the terrible conditions suffered by prisoners, both criminal and political whom the French authorities wanted out of France. We have also visited Japan, the Kamchatka Peninsula in Siberia, up through the Bering Sea to the Aleutian Islands and onwards to the Alaska mainland. Not to be forgotten are the Mediterranean, Adriatic and Baltic Seas visiting all the Baltic capital cities as well as the Norwegian Fjords, Spitsbergen, the North Cape and into Murmansk.

Well my wife did say she would like to travel and see a bit of the world when I retired..............!

At one point it seemed that I may have developed into a bit of a Jonah as far as cruise ships go. Some years ago we were flown from London out to Miami, where we joined the ship *Saga Ruby* on the final leg of her round the world cruise. Many of the passengers had been aboard for the entire cruise, whilst others joined and left at various ports on the way. The penultimate night before returning to Southampton was to be the grand finale gala ball. We were several hundred miles out into the Atlantic Ocean, well to the west of the Bay of Biscay, in what I would describe as 'very heavy weather'. So bad was the motion of the ship that the grand finale and all celebrations were cancelled. Not only that, but a cabin porthole was 'stoved in' by the waves, not only causing cuts and abrasions to a passenger but water damage to her personal belongings as well. The Captain advised all passengers that day to remain in their cabins and food would be brought to them there.

We joined and sailed aboard Fred Olsen's *Boudicca* from Southampton on a wild and wet December evening bound for the Canary Islands. The captain deemed the weather in the Bay of Biscay to be too bad for us to cross, so we spent the next three days lying in the French port of Cherbourg waiting for better sea conditions. As one of the harbour tugs was holding the ship alongside the jetty in the storm force winds, she punched a hole in our ship's side, which of course then had to be repaired before we could sail.

Cunard's *Queen Victoria*, like many of the other new and large cruise liners, uses a propulsion and steering system known as azipods. Azipods or Contra Rotating Propellers (CRP) were originally developed in Finland primarily for use on these large cruise ships. They consist of propulsion units mounted on a steerable pod, suspended vertically down from the ship's bottom. These azipods not only allow ships to be vastly more maneuverable enabling them to travel backward nearly as easily and as fast as they can move forward, but more importantly in these days of economic gloom, they achieve a greater fuel economy as well. Like any new cutting edge system, even though it had been tested exhaustively in test tanks, when applied in the real world, things may not necessarily go as planned. It happened to the *Queen Mary 2* when she was sailing out from Fort Lauderdale in the USA and it happened to the *Queen Victoria* as she was berthing in Malta. It didn't work!

The *Queen Victoria* was not a year old when we joined her in Southampton for a Mediterranean cruise. Part of the itinerary included the ship's first visit to Valletta, capital of the island of Malta. The entrance to the Grand Harbour of Malta is technically difficult at the best of times and, with a strong cross-wind and the huge size of the *Queen Victoria*, entering the port was particularly hazardous. With skilful handling by the local pilot we passed through the narrow tight entrance, and had turned around in order to back the ship into the berth. There was then what we euphemistically call in the business, a "technical" problem. The short answer was that the *Queen Victoria* could not stop! It was terribly embarrassing for all concerned. As she continued to increase sternward speed she made heavy contact with the solid steel and concrete jetty, causing considerable damage to both jetty and holing the ship's stern, fortunately above the waterline. The only consolation may have been that if one is going to have such a mishap and require the services of a ship repair yard, then Malta is one of the best places to be.

With the strategic geographical location of Malta, within the port of Valetta lie numerous ship repair yards and dry docks. Fortunately the *Queen Victoria* did not require dry-docking and so temporary repairs were carried out overnight. This delay meant the cruise schedule had to be altered and, unfortunately, the ship had to miss out the following port of La Goulette in Libya, a port many of the passengers had been looking forward to visiting. She continued her cruise and sailed on until such time as permanent repairs could be carried out. Some weeks later, we saw the *Queen Victoria* once more, and having completed her repairs one would never know just by looking at the ship's stern that anything had ever been amiss.

I was also aboard *QE2* when she was making her final entry into her homeport of Southampton. There she experienced the ignominy of running aground in Southampton water, and was forcibly refloated by a number of local tugs! If the ship owners ever figured out that these incidents occur whilst my wife and I were aboard, would we be invited back I wondered? I guess the Cunard Line never did figure that I might have been a Jonah because they invited me to be the Principle Speaker aboard the maiden voyage of the brand new replacement: *Queen Elizabeth* a couple of years later.

When I found myself in a completely new industry, one of the many things I had to learn was how to find new clients for my speaking engagements. Pure advertising never really worked for me but being invited to speak on BBC local and national radio did. I eventually came to rely on good old fashioned word of mouth and personal recommendations as well as freely distributing top quality brochures. There seems no end to the invitations I now receive from various establishments ashore throughout the length and breadth of the UK and Europe, with many bookings made up to eighteen months in advance.

Looking back on my life and career thus far, I can in all honesty repeat the words I wrote in the preamble to this book, "*I have had a ball*". I am often asked two questions as I continue to travel around the country:

1. Would I do it all again?
2. Have you any regrets?

If you stop and think about the first question, you would realise how silly it is. Because if I were to say 'no' then I have wasted almost 49 years of my life!

Of course I would do it all again, for it has been a wonderful journey, BUT I would only do it again with one proviso; I would want the service as it was and not how it is today.

And now to that second question, do I have any regrets? Well, yes, perhaps there are two.

Firstly, in those heady days of leaving home for the first time and travelling halfway across the world, I thought of nothing else but myself and my future career. Young, innocent, ambitious and totally focussed on 'my dream', I now wish that I had had sufficient maturity and/or sensitivity to realise how much the double impact of my sister's marriage and my departure from New Zealand, all within the space of only five days, would have upon my parents, especially my mother. We were a close-knit family and my mother's life was dedicated to her home, husband and children. That her family effectively disintegrated within only five days, when her eldest daughter was married and her only son left home, was almost too much for her to take. I really do wish that I had thought to say something like "*Thanks Mum, for letting me go*", because I feel sure something as simple as that would have helped to ease her pain.

Secondly, did I have a Jekyll and Hyde character? I don't know. What I do know is that the driven, ambitious young mariner is not someone I would perhaps want to be today. I don't regret my ambitions as such, because I needed them to achieve what I had set out to achieve and at the age I did. But as I look back, I can now see how my single-mindedness may have got in the way of certain aspects of family life. But then, isn't hindsight a wonderful thing?

Now that we are settled into our lovely country home, with a garden my wife spends so many happy hours in, it is hard to envisage my life as it was: sailing the seven seas, flying around the world, living in Africa, The Middle East and the Bahamas; a completely different world.

A NEW FRIEND?

But for my part, whilst I still enjoy making new friends, like the one on the previous page at Gibraltar, as well as meeting, speaking to and entertaining people, whilst I am fit and able to travel, then I shall continue to carry on with what I am doing. As there seems no end to the invitations I continue to receive from various establishments ashore throughout the length and breadth of the UK and Europe it seems I don't have time to 'fall off my perch' just yet!

Having written this book, as well as the training manual when I was stationed in Bahrain, I cannot help but wonder what Miss McGraith, my English teacher, would have had to say - it was she who so graciously awarded me 2% for my 'O' level English language paper and that was, I discovered some time later, for not only writing my name at the top of the paper, but for managing to spell it correctly as well!

For many people the words 'retirement' or 'getting old' simply do not exist, and I am delighted to say I am one of those. The day will of course come when I sail for the last time, heading out to the setting sun. But until it does.........why, life is for both living and enjoying, and long may it continue!

The End

May I now invite you to visit my website:
www.captainwells.co.uk